Rosie Jackson

AF234829

THE WORLD
WILL BECOME
PEACEFUL, BEAUTIFUL
AND ABUNDANT

A compact instruction manual:

150 methods to improve our world

Seraphin Series, Book 3

My deepest gratitude

to the angel

SERAPHIN

for providing me with the

wisdom for this book

My sincere thanks

to everyone who reads this material

and who exerts all practical and mental effort

to put these suggestions into practice,

for you are promoting

SPIRITUAL EVOLUTION

and thus ushering in

A NEW AGE OF PEACE

I also thank my editor, Elisa Lerch,
for the time she has dedicated to this book

Edited by Elisa Lerch
Book cover © Rosie Jackson
from the painting *Descent of the Holy Rain*
Inside illustrations © Rosie Jackson
www.rosiejackson.de
Seraphin Series: Book 3
Seraphin Series: Book 1: *Seraphin's Spirituality School*
Seraphin Series: Book 2: *The Peace Parables*

Bibliografische Information
der Deutschen Nationalbibliothek:
Die Deutsche Nationalbibliothek verzeichnet diese
Publikation in der Deutschen Nationalbibliografie;
detaillierte bibliografische Daten sind im Internet über
http://dnb.dnb.de abrufbar.
Herstellung und Verlag:
BoD – Books on Demand, Norderstedt
1. Auflage Mai 2020
ISBN: 978-3-7519-2066-7

CONTENTS

INTRODUCTION

Our earth has been ravaged by war, conflict, abuse, corruption and desecration for millennia. The great question is: WHAT CAN WE DO TO STOP IT? There are a number of "beliefs" which have been steadily instilled in us, which have led to these tragic circumstances. If we reverse these beliefs, we reverse the situation.

What are these beliefs? First and foremost, we have been led to believe that we are powerless and insignificant, and that we exist on the material plane alone. Various "religions" and rules have been developed to cement our dependence on others. Rigid structures and concepts, notably educational and financial systems, have been developed to keep us confined. Many of us have been programmed to think that there is no life after death, or that we will land in "heaven" or "hell", where we either sit in bliss or burn in pain forever.

In either case, these beliefs are limiting and eradicate any striving to make progress. They stunt our MIND GROWTH. They suggest that our RESPONSIBILITIES will end with death, whereas we are actually on an eternal learning journey through many "lives" and incarnations. Our goal is self-perfection, in order to serve others. This is our greatest joy and fulfilment, and will lead to universal harmony.

The chapters in this book focus on our personal, social, cultural, environmental, global and divine RESPONSIBILITIES. Most important are our divine responsibilities, requiring us to act in alignment with cosmic laws of balance. Simply put, these amount to the law of cause and effect, or the law of one. All thoughts and actions which we send out into the world have an effect. It is our responsibility to ensure the quality of those thoughts and actions. The law of one ensures that the energy we emit returns to us. In other words, we reap what we sow. The "golden rule" is that we should do unto others as we wish to be treated ourselves.

Over time, many enlightened masters, including Jesus, have been assigned here by universal administration to "uplift" the vibration of our earth. They have attempted to teach "another way" – living in alignment with these laws and developing a very personal relationship with the Divine ("The Kingdom of God is within us"). It is time for us to reclaim this, our divine sovereignty, independent of outside influences, and to communicate with our divine inner advisor in order to overthrow the shackles of the past. Thus will we turn into our own religious gurus, our own policeman, our own judge, and "government". Resting securely in ourselves, always independent and perfectly balanced, we will recover our boundless creativity, and we will consciously construct a PEACEFUL, BEAUTIFUL AND ABUNDANT WORLD.

How can the world become peaceful, beautiful and abundant? Many of these answers are the result of "intuitive, medial writing". Many have also been received telepathically from the angel, Seraphin. More detailed texts and original messages from Seraphin can be found in the book SERAPHIN'S SPIRITUALITY SCHOOL. May all the readers and users of this book be showered with abundant blessings on their spiritual path. Rosie Jackson.

THE PURPOSE OF THIS BOOK

This is a concise instruction manual on how to transform our earth. Each section can be used for individual or group work:

GROUP EXERCISE

1. A teacher and students sit together in a circle.

2. The teacher reads the first sentence out loud, for example "The world will become peaceful, beautiful and abundant IF WE TRANSCEND THE PAST"

3. All students go into meditation for a few minutes, reflecting on this sentence.

4. Each student in turn has three minutes to share what they have "seen" and felt during meditation. No one comments or discusses. If the student runs out of things to say, and if the three minutes are not

yet over, the group is required to sit in silence for the remaining time.

5. The teacher reads the rest of the section pertaining to the original sentence.

6. Each student in turn expresses their further thoughts for three minutes. No one discusses

7. Group discussion

8. Each student in turn says "The world will become peaceful, beautiful and abundant if I …" and completes the sentence immediately without hesitating. Group discussion can follow.

PERSONAL EXERCISE

Readers of this book are invited to write "The world will become peaceful, beautiful and abundant if I", and complete the sentence immediately.

This can be written every morning to set personal goals for the day, and every evening to promote reflection on one's own behaviour during the day.

CHAPTER 1

OUR RESPONSIBILITY
TO REGULATE OUR
BEHAVIOUR

**The world will become
peaceful, beautiful and abundant**

IF WE LOOK INTO EACH OTHER'S EYES

How often do we look into each other's eyes? Turning away is a rampant disease, for example on long commutes in urban areas, where every spare moment appears to be consumed by mobile phones, the internet or social media.

Our attention is not on our surroundings. Most heads are always DOWN, and we do not notice if someone needs help. We are unable to return a smile. We are unable to give up a seat to a disabled person on a train. We are unable to benefit from new, inspiring encounters. We are distracted and unable to react quickly to danger.

To look directly into someone's eyes is to show them respect, give them attention, and sometimes to see "the window to the soul". It is this very personal connection which will strengthen our bonds with friends and strangers alike.

Imagine what would happen if we went through a ritual every time we meet someone new: we could hold both their hands in silence, and look deep into their eyes for three minutes. Then we could say to each other "I GREET THE DIVINE IN YOU".

**The world will become
peaceful, beautiful and abundant**

IF EVERYONE PAUSES TO THINK
BEFORE THEY SPEAK

Counting to 5, before responding to someone who is irritating us or angering us, can prevent us from following our usual patterns of behaviour in our relationships with others. It can prevent us from being triggered and "blowing our top". Exploding inexplicably is an OVER-REACTION. If we count to five, we can spare our friends and families the outbursts for which our own hang-ups or untreated "wounds" are responsible.

The most successful managers are those which talk the least. This means that they are direct, clear and focussed. How can we improve our clarity when we talk? How can we develop into sensitive, good listeners? One method is to reduce the other senses. If we want to listen better, we can lie in a dark room in silence for 3 hours, and then play a beautiful piece of music. We will learn to appreciate silence, and we will listen to music like never before.

If we spend a weekend blindfold, with visual stimuli removed, we notice every incomplete sentence and every superfluous word. We notice how words are used to flatter or make excuses. Thus, we refine our listening skills and are much more careful about which words WE decide to utter.

**The world will become
peaceful, beautiful and abundant**

IF WE THROW AWAY THE PROPS AND SMILE

Life offers a vast field of experimentation. One revolutionary experiment is to

SMILE AT EVERYONE WE MEET FOR ONE DAY,

and see what difference it makes. Even this, the simplest of creative acts - which is possible for everyone - may cause consternation. If the mere suggestion conjures up fears of "what if", we are already fearfully contemplating the reactions.

Communicating in a friendly, authentic and spontaneous manner can replace the props of modern society which help people get over their fear of approaching each other. What are these props? One example is clubs with loud music which encourage a lot of body contact and discourage conversation. Other props include alcohol which "relaxes" and drugs which make us "high". Another prop is shopping experiences for clothes where the focus is on outer shows of appearance rather than communication from the "inside".

If we pull all these props away, we are left with the "naked" soul. We no longer cover anything up. We are left with the opportunity for authentic, individual self-expression.

**The world will become
peaceful, beautiful and abundant**

IF WE TREAT EVERYONE WE ENCOUNTER WITH CONSIDERATION

If we assume we "know" someone, and if we treat them in a dismissive or "over-familiar" way, we have already lost. We should not cage someone in, judging solely by our own perceptions.

If someone appears to be coming from a different direction than ourselves, with contradictory ideas, this what we are perceiving, but this view is not necessarily "truth".

In order to better understand our fellow human beings (instead of remaining stagnant in the pond of our own limited knowing), it is necessary to listen.

After listening, it is also necessary to ask many questions: then we can understand their experiences, feelings and motivations. Then we can get a clearer picture of what might help or inspire them.

**The world will become
peaceful, beautiful and abundant**

IF WE SHOW COURTESY, GRATITUDE AND COMPASSIONATE HONESTY

These three qualities, if consistently manifested by all, would change the face of the planet in an instant - especially if we add "trust in the Divine" to the list.

It is not possible to go into conflict with someone we respect. War cannot be conducted between those who show each other mutual courtesy. Lies and manipulation cannot arise if everything is openly and honestly discussed. And if we show gratitude, more experiences for which we are grateful will inevitably come our way.

Such are the laws of attraction. What we give, we receive. If we are honest, others are more likely to be honest with us. If we are respectful, we are more likely to earn respect. Through our behaviour, we can determine which response and what sort of society we prefer – peaceful conviviality or painful strife.

Honesty is sometimes a two-edged sword: it should not be brutal, but compassionate: we should not present the "naked truth" to those who are fragile and over-burdened. This may cause them to shut down completely, or to collapse under the weight.

Just as we are fed truth in digestible portions, so do we also hand out digestible portions of the truth to others. This sort of honesty can be referred to as "compassionate honesty", for to reveal all would not necessarily further the individual's path, but rather create a blockage, resulting in severe stagnation.

**The world will become
peaceful, beautiful and abundant**

IF WE DEVELOP PATIENCE WHERE IT IS DUE

Lack of patience is sometimes related to overriding ego. We might like to be the "star of the show". We might like to impress others around us. We may like to soak in admiration. Convinced of our superiority, or striving to achieve it, we interrupt others to make ourselves noticed, or to make sure that our self-interested motivations are not overlooked.

We write excessive "memos" to our bosses, stating our rights and point of view. We waste time, creating a war on paper, thinking we are at great odds with each other, when what we actually did was refuse to hear the other person out.

We cannot be patient, and hear another out, if we are full of anger or resentment. We cannot rationally and measuredly assess a situation if we are coloured by hate and prejudice. As always, it is our mandate to research into the real source of these outbursts in ourselves, to discover the hurts and wounds which have left us sensitive, and which lead us to over-react if triggered. We are often not under attack: we are simply approached. It is the unhealed wound which perceives - erroneously - that we are under attack.

Only when we have cleared all these burdens from our past will we be able to encounter others with fairness, allowing them to tell their story without interruption, so that we can better understand the real picture. Impatience is an overall term for not being able to wait.

How patient are we? Of course, we are justified in interrupting if we encounter violence or error, but often it is just a reflection of our unprocessed feelings.

How difficult is it for us to listen to someone who immediately irritates us? How much of other people's history are we unaware - all of which culminates in this very moment?

How do we wish others to treat us when we are impassioned to speak our mind? May we all improve our patience, for it is a way of learning more.

**The world will become
peaceful, beautiful and abundant**

IF WE DO NOT IMMEDIATELY JUDGE

Think of all the words which immediately make our hackles rise, and which immediately make us condemn someone. What is our inner reaction if we hear that someone is a

COMMUNIST or a CONSPIRACY THEORIST?

We have an astonishing tendency to categorise before we know someone, and even when we think we know someone, can we really know their inner thoughts? Might we only understand the real purpose of someone's life in the very final moments of recognition before their death? What would change if we looked for similarities rather than differences? How are beggars, kings, teachers, toddlers, animals great and small

ALL THE SAME?

They all thrive on love.

Is there anyone who really knows our inner thoughts? The answer is YES. Our inner godly core or "fragment" or "advisor" KNOWS EVERYTHING WE THINK, and is therefore in an excellent position to GIVE US THE RIGHT ADVICE. This advisor does not judge us, but loves us unconditionally, irrespective of which direction we choose to take.

**The world will become
peaceful, beautiful and abundant**

IF EVERYONE RECOGNISES THAT WHAT THEY SEE IS A MIRROR OF THEMSELVES

The process of projection is generally in play. This means that what we have already experienced - the joys and the pains - influences the way we perceive other people. If we meet someone new, we might take an instant dislike to them, though others may find them totally amiable. This does not have to do with the person in question, though there are undoubtedly more pleasant and less pleasant personal traits which we can agree upon. For example: if you perceive that an elderly man is speaking to you harshly, you may take an instant dislike to this person. This "overreaction" is not necessarily due to what has just been said, but because it triggers unpleasant memories of what your father or some other person in authority said to you in the past.

The "mirror principle" works both ways. If we dislike a person for being "uncommunicative", this is an invitation to take a long hard look at our own lack of communication. There will always be something to learn if we understand this. We recognise WHAT WE ARE FAMILIAR WITH, as opposed to what might really be in front of our eyes. If we realise this, so many strained encounters will become relaxed, and much can be seen in a new and peaceful light.

The world will become
peaceful, beautiful and abundant

IF WE INCREASE THE QUALITY WE PERCEIVE IS LACKING IN OTHERS

Realising that we are PROJECTING can be an intense shock. Here is an example: we may seem justified in screaming and shouting rude comments if someone suddenly touches our neck.

However, if that person is not going for the jugular vein and is actually trying to give us a hug, a past experience is "interfering" with the present, for example, if someone nearly strangled us in our childhood.

This is how past experiences can cloud the present. Once this is understood, we may see that the other person is not "at fault", and that we ourselves contribute to misunderstandings.

When we understand this, we will go through our whole lives again, pinpointing all occasions when we felt wronged or angry, and we will discover how we were partly responsible.

With time, we will learn to discern whether an unpleasant incident arises from deliberate provocation, or whether it is a result of our own "over-reactions".

**The world will become
peaceful, beautiful and abundant**

IF EVERYTHING IS PROCESSED IMMEDIATELY

We often tend to "dither" if we perceive something as being unpleasant. It helps if we keep our goal firmly in mind. Then it will be immediately obvious whether the opportunities presented to us are actually opportunities, spurring us on towards our goal, or whether they are merely distractions, designed to test us.

ABSOLUTE CLARITY OF PURPOSE MAKES CHOOSING A SIMPLE PROCESS.

We are "in the flow" if every experience is processed, looked at briefly, appreciated for its lesson and then

RELEASED.

If every incident or encounter is immediately processed before nightfall, the heavy traces of resentful memories will no longer take their toll on our skin.

Instead of worn and weary faces, we will eternally wear the expression of youth.

**The world will become
peaceful, beautiful and abundant**

IF WE TRANSCEND THE PAST

Many of us live our lives by looking through the veil of the past, which is a narrowed view. This severely darkens our vision. This inhibits our dreams. This limits our possibilities. For many of us, the past is something which is still incredibly VIBRANT AND ALIVE - something which VALIDATES our present existence, and something which we must "live up to". But to break with the past may well be positive, as we are thereby throwing off the shackles which ensnare our imagination.

To search through past experiences for possible answers to our present difficulties is to embark upon a perilous journey. We must focus on the present. We are presently MOVING THROUGH COMPLETELY DIFFERENT WATERS. Previous solutions to small storms will not be adequate for coping with a current LARGE STORM.

Imagine that we have a very small suitcase, and that it has no room for things of the past, including all behaviours which have caused us distress or which have led to an undesirable life. This suitcase is not for sad memories. It is intended as a showcase for the future, and for our ideas about how to create a wonderful and peaceful world. We can imagine carrying this suitcase around with us as we go through our lives.

**The world will become
peaceful, beautiful and abundant**

IF WE ARE COURAGEOUS TO THE CORE

How often do we feel hesitation when we travel to new places, enter into new relationships, or face new experiences? Do we "dive into" new experiences, or do we move forwards and - at the same time - hold back, resulting in inner conflict and preventing full commitment. This is not a recommendation to dive recklessly and naively into servitude, but to walk confidently in our chosen direction.

It is our task to discover what is holding us back from entering into a new project joyfully, with enthusiasm and dedication. Sometimes we are hurt by previous experiences and are therefore wary of new ones. This means that we are PROJECTING our past onto the present, and this may distort our view of the present. Other obstacles to moving forward are

OBJECTS, PEOPLE AND CIRCUMSTANCES
WHICH WE DO NOT WANT TO LEAVE BEHIND.

In such cases, closure is required before progress can be made.

How can we be "courageous to the core"? If we frequently converse with the divine part INSIDE OURSELVES, then we will intuitively KNOW which direction is the right one, and we will know that there can be no mistake about our choice. If we, in our very "core", are confident about this, we will always move forward courageously. And if the new experience should "disappoint" us, it is not for us to point our fingers at our Divine advisors for proposing something unpleasant: it is up to us to RECOGNISE that this unpleasant experience is part of a learning lesson which - once learnt - will be the STEPPING STONE TO HIGHER THINGS.

The world will become
peaceful, beautiful and abundant

IF WE LEARN TRUE TRUST

True trust is everlasting. Short-lived periods of trust are of little use. Time is the element which enables deep trust to develop over eras of uncertainty.

If we have an overview over long periods of time, we start to realise that our past experiences were necessary for our own development. We develop trust in this process, even when facing very difficult situations.

Tracking our lives over long periods also shows us all the inexplicable opportunities and encounters which occurred "by chance". These are placed in our path by Divine hand. When we know without a doubt that we are divinely guided, our trust becomes unshakeable and ever-present. This means that even if someone is well-disposed towards us, or dishonest to us, we may trust that this is the right experience for us at that particular time.

The world will become
peaceful, beautiful and abundant

IF WE PRACTICE TRUE HUMILITY

Nature can supply us with many good examples of "humility". Trees do not strive to impress each other. Water does not aim to succeed. Seeds do not give parties when they germinate, flower or die. They are providers of food but expect no payment. Birds manage to get through life without spending any money. They do not compete for "likes" on social media. They do not retreat "on holiday" because they think they need a rest. Neither do they retire because they have reached a certain age. They only stop when their natural cycle has come to an end, and they end without pomp and circumstance.

While parties and celebrations can be a wonderful way of bringing people together and honouring passage, how much of this is pandering to ego, and what happens when attempts to sustain ego fail? The higher the pride, the steeper the fall.

The world will become
peaceful, beautiful and abundant

IF WE RETAIN ETERNAL, CENTRAL REPOSE

We may experience dreadful situations which can shake or break us. Whether we regard these incidents or encounters as tragic, or simply fleeting lessons which are specifically designed for our optimal learning, is our personal choice.

To REALISE this, rather than feeling that we must succumb to a set of unpleasant circumstances, is the path to constant repose.

ONCE WE HAVE ACHIEVED THIS STATE OF COMPOSURE, NOTHING CAN DISTURB IT.

All obstacles provide perfect practice in this discipline. They may shake us, but if we KNOW where our divine centre is, then we can always return to it.

To remain in balance is to contribute to planetary balance.

CHAPTER 2

OUR RESPONSIBILITY
TO KEEP LEARNING

**The world will become
peaceful, beautiful and abundant**

IF WE REGARD OBSTACLES AS CHANCES TO MOVE FORWARD

When we encounter barriers, our momentum is initially decreased. We may examine these barriers deciding – whether consciously or subconsciously – whether to accept them, or whether it is possible to destroy them. We can assess their quality. Or we may ignore them.

It is beneficial to regard them as

HINDRANCES WHICH HELP US TO MOVE FORWARD TOWARDS A MORE INSPIRED AND DIVINE PATH OF VOCATION.

We may lose faith or confidence. We may seek to retrieve them through magic formulas, rituals, books, drugs or groups which promise speedy forward progression.

Yet progress can only be made by OURSELVES, by increasing our critical abilities and inner strength, using each encounter and obstacle to learn and to move upwards.

Even in the most terrible of circumstances, this can be so. There is always a "silver lining".

**The world will become
peaceful, beautiful and abundant**

IF WE TAKE ENOUGH TIME TO THINK DEEPLY

Some people may pause for moments of reflection, but often these do not go deep enough. A small hiatus of calm and contemplation (which might occur during weekends or "holiday") brings but little new insight. It is simply a short period of non-action and rest which bolsters up the strength to continue with the "normal" routine, which we try to survive by thinking about the next superficial "break". This does not penetrate the shadows. Subconsciously, people are afraid of what they might find lurking in those same shadows.

How can real insights be gained?

By deliberately setting time aside regularly to delve deep into the shadows and to meet the ensuing challenges.

Meditation, yoga, deep breathing retreats and group therapy are some of the possible methods of discovering and overcoming that which lurks below the surface.

Once personal "obstacles" have been overcome, our eyes are opened to a more intensive way of living: we will no longer have to take "time out" to think deeply, because we will be doing it all the time.

**The world will become
peaceful, beautiful and abundant**

IF WE DO NOT RUN ON AUTOMATIC

We all have certain habits, beliefs, customs, convictions and experiences which colour our immediate reactions to other people, or to words being said.

How much of our conversation is actually original, in the sense of original new thoughts, as opposed to trotting out lots of old concepts, copied phrases and worn out strategies? In fact, how are we to react to someone appropriately, whether we think we know them well or not?

This is difficult because everything is always changing. There is no logical or obvious way of "knowing" exactly what stage a person is in. They may have just undergone a transformation, or suffered some blow. They may need a completely new form of inspiration or assistance.

This is where our GODLY INTUITION comes in. This ADAPTS to the situation, each time anew. The GODLY CORE WITHIN US will tell us how to approach someone, what they need, if there are any dangers, what it is possible to talk about, and what information we should withhold at that specific time. It will also tell us to STOP TALKING, if that is the best stance at that particular time.

If we are connected to this source of wisdom within, if we listen to this small, still voice and act accordingly, then we will

NEVER RUN ON AUTOMATIC.

We will be running according to divine advice, which is always specifically and specially crafted for the listener. This advice will ultimately benefit all who act upon it, and all who are on the receiving end of our inspired action.

**The world will become
peaceful, beautiful and abundant**

IF WE DEPROGRAMME OURSELVES

Spiders spin their webs with great dedication, care and precision, because their lives and growth depends upon it. Do spiders spend hours at their school desks, chewing their pencils, straining to digest streams of information, attempting to assimilate all facts presented to them on a convenient plate so that - in the end - they might receive full marks in an examination? Do spiders apply for planning permission or pay fees or take out credit before building their home? What is our innate "unlearnt" programming? How have we been negatively "programmed?

We have been led to think that we will only survive if we have lots of money: success is ensured if we are completely independent and share with no one.

We have been led to believe that if we are ill, medicine will cure us, and if we do not work, "welfare" will take care of us.

We are led to believe that "entertainment" will cure boredom. We are led to believe that if our body looks perfect, we will find the perfect mate.

We have been programmed to believe that it is open-minded to tolerate excesses, and that "rights" must be fought for, even if this involves violence.

We have been led to think that sacredness is "uncool" and that living "happily ever after" involves no work on oneself.

We have been led to believe that we are alone in the universe, and that we are the only civilization which has inhabited this planet.

We have been led to believe that traditional family life and marriage are old-fashioned and obsolete, thus encroaching on all children's emotional stability and security.

Worst of all, we have let ourselves become convinced that war is a justifiable means of "self-defence". If we de-programme all this, we will be able to move forward.

The world will become
peaceful, beautiful and abundant

IF WE JOURNEY IN EVER-WIDENING CIRCLES

When light falls on a large lake which is swept by wind, the sun glitters on the constantly changing contours of the waves. This constant mix of potential and possibilities of form is ours to grasp, ours to embrace, ours to connect with in ever-varying ways, in order to expand our minds, our experiences and our contributions to the whole.

We are pebbles which land in the waters of a still lake. Even if the pebble is very small, it creates huge circles of ripples in every direction. We affect the whole with every breath. If we continue our various journeys in ever-widening circles, always experiencing new depths through our openness, we will increase our contribution, our exhilaration and our joy.

**The world will become
peaceful, beautiful and abundant**

**IF WE GO INTO ACTION INSTEAD OF
HIDING BEHIND WORDS**

How often are our statements of good intent, our suggestions for improvement, our resolutions by international bodies, or the mission statements of companies or individuals ACTUALLY CARRIED OUT? Or does it take weeks, or a year, or twenty years before they are actually put into effect?

Why do we procrastinate?

Why do we allow ourselves to be diverted, un-focussed and redirected? Sometimes this is due to "adverse circumstances" which we consider too challenging to face.

Sometimes we are corrupted by those who wish to keep us in a passive stance. We often release good intentions because we are told that it does not matter. This is a sign of declining moral standards. Do we do what we say? Do we mean what we say? And does it matter if we don't do what we say?

If we do not do what we say, how can TRUST BETWEEN INDIVIDUALS AND NATIONS GROW? If no one is reliable, ON WHOM CAN WE RELY? Without mutual trust, stability cannot arise. If we all act with honest integrity AND STAND BY OUR WORD, then stability and peace will flourish.

**The world will become
peaceful, beautiful and abundant**

**IF WE KEEP ON TRACK DESPITE
ATTEMPTS TO DISRUPT US**

Many of us have "dreams" of what we want to achieve in a "perfect world". Often, we are deterred because the world simply is not perfect. Yet we fail to realise that our chosen path – in combination with the chosen paths of all other inhabitants on this earth – determines the level of perfection on this planet. Our every thought and action contributes to – or detracts from - the overall picture.

If we become increasingly aware of our POWER TO MAKE A DIFFERENCE, we will simultaneously become more aware of ALL OBSTACLES IN OUR PATH. Sometimes we are stopped by

DELIBERATE, PRE-MEDITATED AGGRESSION.

Sometimes we allow others to steal our time or change our priorities. Sometimes we INTERRUPT OURSELVES during important missions because of personal weaknesses or laziness.

Self-discipline is often a battle with ourselves. If we are always aware of the IMPORTANCE of our mission, however – if we write it on our mirror so that we see it every morning, and if we state it daily, requesting celestial assistance – we will inevitably travel towards it.

**The world will become
peaceful, beautiful and abundant**

IF WE CONTINUALLY CHECK GROWTH AND KEEP EVERYTHING IN VIEW

Checking growth (not curbing or controlling or manipulating it) is extremely important. It requires SUPERVISION AND GUIDANCE IN A GODLY DIRECTION.

This is what an ideal education system does – guide bright and eager minds to the fulfilment of their great potential, WHILE STILL MAINTAINING RELATIONSHIPS WITH OTHERS.

Joint or "co-creative" projects will function well if everyone is completely involved. Ideally, the best is brought out in everyone by everyone.

While making personal contributions, everyone should simultaneously retain an overview, even if it is only out of the corner of their eye. This is why CIRCLES (for example circular tables or seating arrangements) are so important. Everyone is thus energetically included.

In group discussion, it may sometimes be detrimental and time-consuming to follow up on all suggestions or comments. However, a smooth path can be assured if we are constantly aware of the feelings of all participants, since to ignore them may result in future upheaval on a major scale.

**The world will become
peaceful, beautiful and abundant**

**IF WE STOP IGNORING VIOLENCE,
UGLINESS AND DESECRATION.**

Many people prefer to "keep the peace". This desire might prevent them from taking deliberate action in unpleasant situations.

Sometimes, "keeping the peace" is only superficial. It does not destroy the roots of evil. If we ignore ugly situations, as well as ugly places, we may deceive ourselves into thinking that our lives are harmonious and beautiful, yet this will only be a pleasant veneer.

The cosmic law of balance will ensure that imbalances are redressed, therefore all that which is suppressed and hidden will actually come into view at a later stage, and we will be forced to give it our undivided attention.

We will be urged to find solutions, not just for our immediate surroundings, but worldwide.

**The world will become
peaceful, beautiful and abundant**

IF WE REMEMBER TO ENCOMPASS ALL IN OUR VISION

Sometimes we may choose to dive into pits of depression. Sometimes we may choose to be overwhelmed by circumstances. Sometimes - if we are in love, for example - we choose to forget everything, and to ride exclusively on waves of delight. Yet beauty is actually always to be found - in the smallest flower, for example. To encompass all in our vision is to be balanced and capable of measured action.

**The world will become
peaceful, beautiful and abundant**

IF EVERYONE RESEMBLES A DIAMOND

We all have a divine core. A diamond does not shine in its original state. A diamond-cutter will hold it up to the light and look at it from all angles in order to see how it can be cut best. Only then does the diamond cutter start to pare away. We should be aware of our intrinsic value and divinity, even if this is not obvious to outsiders. Our task is to work at ourselves so that we sparkle and shine, and reach our full potential. This is our journey - to develop the best in ourselves and move from darkness to light.

**The world will become
peaceful, beautiful and abundant**

IF WE LEARN TO FALL AND FALL TO LEARN

Small babies learning to walk have no fear of falling – it is all part of the natural process of trying to walk. If they do not succeed, they simply try again. They have no shame about how many times they might fall over. No one gets angry about how many times they do. Babies are undaunted, and eventually they learn to keep their balance.

BALANCE IS NOT POSSIBLE WITHOUT EXPERIENCING THE FALL.

To fall as an adult often evokes responses of "How could that happen?" or "This is impossible!" or "I must have made a fool of myself".

Falling is no longer seen as a natural process which encourages offers of help from friendly hands, but as a failure.

The harder the ground we fall upon, and the greater the injury, the longer we are forced to lie down and consider why it is necessary to STOP AND THINK.

If we ignore this chance, then "soul desire" will organise something of even greater impact to increase the potency of the wake-up call.

What is FALLING TO LEARN? When we regard accidents as "stepping stones", we learn to see them as the next necessary stage of our learning process. This may cause temporary pain, but later it will fill us with gratitude because we recognize it as something which propelled us forward.

**The world will become
peaceful, beautiful and abundant**

**IF EVERYONE KNOWS
THAT THEY DO NOT KNOW**

A ladybird is running across the skin of your finger. What does she understand about you? She explores the surface of your skin, travelling over fingernails and hairs. She may discover that the five fingers she traverses are connected, or she may see them as 5 separate pinks hills, according to whether she hops from one to another, or whether she runs to each fingertip and back, starting from the palm of your hand. In effect, she knows very little of your essence, though she may acquire a more accurate impression of your size if she spreads her wings and flies, thus viewing you from a greatly expanded perspective.

Understanding someone is a lengthy process. Many people fall into the trap of immediately judging someone according to what they once said or did. We can never "know" anyone. Also, everyone is continually EVOLVING, as we are always EVOLVING. Each encounter between two people is a momentary affair, without ever having the "full picture". If we are aware of this, then our journey is full of WONDER as we contemplate what NEW ASPECTS of a person will come to light today, or how we may be invited to REVISE OUR PREVIOUS OPINION.

The world will become
peaceful, beautiful and abundant

IF WE REMEMBER THERE IS
SO MUCH MORE WE DONT KNOW

We are often so convinced about our own opinion. It is based on facts and situations we have experienced at first hand and which have affected us deeply. Yet these occurred at a certain time between certain people of certain mind-sets, under certain influences, and all these perimeters have the potential for change in a single second. So if we find ourselves in difficulties, we can step back, take a deep breath and say the following to ourselves:

REMEMBER THERE ARE
SO MANY PLACES TO GO,

REMEMBER THERE ARE
SO MANY SEASONS TO GROW,

REMEMBER THERE ARE
SO MANY THINGS WE DON'T KNOW.

**The world will become
peaceful, beautiful and abundant**

IF WE RECOGNISE THE END

Do we recognize when the end is near, or do we stoically continue until we ram our heads against a brick wall? What are the signs that we have reached the end?

We may discover bones as we clear away rubble. We may suddenly discover refuse on supposedly pristine lawns (or corruption in supposedly pristine minds, or unthinkable evil goals in "charitable" organisations). The clues will fall into our hands. Will we wonder where they have come from, or why they have not fallen into our hands before?

The road to the end is littered with clues, whether it is the end of a relationship, the end of a career, or the end of a global era. The end is near if those who take outnumber those who give. The end is near if those who sleep outnumber those who are awake.

How quick are we to recognize that we are at a DEAD END and that our collective behaviour has brought us to this point?

The secret is to WAKE UP before the damage is done. The secret is to ALWAYS BE AWARE OF EVIL, DISHONESTY AND CORRUPTION AND TO NIP IT IN THE BUD, whether it is in OURSELVES or IN OTHERS.

**The world will become
peaceful, beautiful and abundant**

IF WE TRACK OUR ACTIVITIES

If we take a long, hard look at how we spend the 24 hours of our day, how many of those hours are spent in a "profitable" way, not in the sense of HOW MUCH MONEY DID I EARN IN THAT HOUR, but in the sense of DID I SPEND THAT HOUR TO ASSIST SOMEONE, OR TO IMPROVE A BAD SITUATION, OR TO UPLIFT THE VIBRATION OF THE EARTH? Or did I spend that particular hour procrastinating, recovering from some self-inflicted excess, living in a virtual reality or swallowing "entertainment"?

Just as we periodically throw rubbish out of our rooms/flats/houses, we should similarly periodically "clean out" our lives and our MINDS, in order to accelerate our joy and fulfilment.

How can this be achieved? By TRACKING OURSELVES, writing down what we do, what we eat, where we go, how often we rest, how long we sleep, what we buy, when we are doing something useful.

Tracking oneself is not a method of JUDGEMENT - it is simply WRITING THINGS DOWN to increase our awareness.

After a week of writing things down, we can re-read our notes. We will more clearly see our habits, successes and failings. A pattern will emerge, and because we are increasingly AWARE OF THESE PATTERNS, they are increasingly easy to change. Thus, we will become more effective, happier, and more loving to ourselves and others.

The world will become
peaceful, beautiful and abundant

IF WE RECOGNISE THE GREAT TEACHERS AMONG US

This earth has several great teachers at present, and has been blessed with several great teachers in the past. Their common trait is that they have the welfare of the entire globe at heart.

How can we find them? We must increase our discernment, discovering who is trying to pull the wool over our eyes, who is trying to distract us, who is trying to manipulate us, who is trying to mock and paralyze us, and who is genuinely trying to make us look "outside the box". Then we will discover who is genuinely trying to EMPOWER AND ENLIGHTEN US. With this acquired wisdom, we can better understand ourselves, others, and that which is GREATER THAN OURSELVES:

GOD, ALLAH, THE ONE, THE CREATION, UNIVERSAL CONSCIOUSNESS, COSMIC MIND - or whatever term you prefer.

CHAPTER 3

OUR RESPONSIBILITY
TO MANIFEST OUR VISIONS

The world will become
peaceful, beautiful and abundant

IF BEAUTIFUL THOUGHTS ARE ACTED UPON

Suppose you have a beautiful thought?

Think of one such thought - something which is extremely attractive for you or for someone else - a surprise party, or a pet project, or a way to connect two or more people.

Let us take the "surprise party" as an example. You can imagine how wonderful it would be to surprise someone you love dearly. You can keep it all in your head if you like. That is your choice.

However, if you mention it to someone else, especially someone who is positive and active (again, your choice who to talk to), then probably there will be a synergy effect – an explosion of new ideas. The more you talk about this "beautiful thought", the more it develops, and the more it MANIFESTS IN REALITY.

And then the day of the surprise party arrives and it is a tremendous success,

ALL BECAUSE YOU ACTED UPON THAT BEAUTIFUL THOUGHT.

**The world will become
peaceful, beautiful and abundant**

IF WE TRY TO TURN OUR VISIONS INTO REALITY

In our present society, many people wish to escape from "harsh reality", and indeed it is necessary to find peace in some way, after being confronted with situations which degrade, abuse and deject.

This might provide "light relief", yet in the long run this will not actually change the "harsh reality" we are trying to avoid. This is only achieved if we look it in the eye, identifying exactly how it was created, and considering which part of it we can change.

We are all much more powerful than we think. We can use every thought, word and action - like building bricks - to construct something new: there is a wealth of unexploited potential WITHIN EVERY PERSON.

The value of virtual realities (which do not involve power, greed or corruption) is that they can act as forerunners of what can be changed on earth. These are "visions of a better future".

If we implement these, putting energy into them in a consistent and dedicated manner, this will have a positive effect, even if everything around us temporarily points to the contrary.

**The world will become
peaceful, beautiful and abundant**

IF HUMANS RISE ABOVE THEIR PRESENT CONCEPT OF THEMSELVES

How many times do we say "I'M ONLY HUMAN AFTER ALL", in order to excuse some weakness and to indicate our fragility. This is similar to saying "THE SPIRIT IS WILLING, BUT THE FLESH IS WEAK", meaning we want to act in an exemplary matter, but we cannot find the energy or willpower.

These are excuses. All changes take place on a mental plane first. If this is not accomplished, there will be no change in the physical. The "decider" is not our body. This is merely our present vehicle for the transport of spirit. We will exchange it for another, once this life is over.

What is the difference between humans and animals? Humans are capable of GAINING WISDOM and of SHOWING WORSHIP. Humans are capable of SELF DEVELOPMENT AND LEARNING. Only some of the higher animals are in this sort of league - those who develop love, trust and dedication, e.g. dogs, cats and horses. So what are humans actually? They are SOULS housed in a HUMAN BODY entrusted with a DIVINE TASK which they are to discover during their journey, ever striving towards godly perfection. When humans fully accept this concept of themselves, all people will live fruitfully fulfilling their divine missions.

**The world will become
peaceful, beautiful and abundant**

IF WE GO BEYOND THE BOUNDARIES OF THE FAMILIAR

Ideally, we should look everything straight in the eye, in full awareness of our surroundings, of our safely concealed thoughts, of our unexpressed resentment and of our unexpressed LOVE.

Sometimes it seems impossible to love a criminal, yet however horrific a crime may be, we can also consider that we are not yet privy to a further enlightening perspective.

It is easy to stargaze, but the more we drift, the greater the shock when we hit reality. The more we fail to investigate, the more appalled or delighted we will be when we are forced to open our eyes. The longer we sleep, the greater the wake-up call.

We should not allow "truth" to be presented to us conveniently on a plate, always coloured by the same perspective, always flavoured by the same familiar and reassuring condiments, always at the same temperature for exactly the same tastes.

Going beyond the boundaries of the familiar will serve us well. If we clean dark corners, we will throw out the cobwebs of neglect and the dust of resignation to discover our inner wealth.

Our wellbeing will depend on the degree of our authenticity, and on the intensity with which we have searched out our "shadow worlds". In so doing, we will retrieve our own biographies, reclaim our divinity, and realign our purpose with the Divine.

**The world will become
peaceful, beautiful and abundant**

IF WE CAN IMAGINE THE IMPOSSIBLE

Can we imagine the "impossible", or is our "mind development" strangled? Can we imagine that the waves of the sea suddenly freeze in motion? Can we imagine that everything we believe is untrue? Can we imagine that we are actually huge, enlightened beings, temporarily encased in a shell called the "human body", for the purpose of experience and assisting others? Can we imagine our world as a perfectly ordered member of a perfectly ordered universe? Can we imagine peace on earth?

Sustained dedication, devotion and spiritual advance will earn us access to other worlds, other technologies and other possibilities. Imagination and our creativity are of paramount importance. Instead of being content with ready-made choices, we are called upon to invent and create. To be truly responsible and live our very individual and unique talents, we must follow our own vocation. Also, we will create our own personal spiritual path, instead of selecting from a palette of religions which distort the true message of the masters who set them into motion.

What will set us into motion? Will we stop but for a moment to contemplate the huge range of possibilities rather than soldier on bravely through our particular daily grind? As in all acute situations, the grind will come to a halt, forcing us to consider these same issues from a place of stillness and silence. And after experiencing depths we thought were impossible, we will be able to imagine the heights which we thought were impossible.

**The world will become
peaceful, beautiful and abundant**

**IF WE KNOW WHAT TO KEEP AND WHAT TO
DESTROY WHILE CREATING OUR DREAM**

Making changes can be a challenging process, whether we are renovating a building, the world, or ONESELF. It requires careful consideration of the following questions:

Are the changes you make cosmetic or radical?
What do you chose to modify or destroy?
How much of the old do you leave standing?
How quickly do you throw something away?
How often does indecision hamper progress?
Do unpleasant discoveries set you back?

Do you retain an overall perspective,
or do you lose yourself in detail?
Do you consciously preserve that which is strong?
Do you hold on to flimsy structures/relationships
although they are weak?
Are you doing this for yourself or others?
Is this a co-creative effort, or one person's project
carried out by minions?
How easily are you led by other's opinions?
How often do you allow experts in their field to
state their view?
How quickly do you recognise your own limits?
How often do you follow your intuition or vision
without question?
How quickly do you back down from your ideals?
Is this due to practical common sense,
or desire to please another?
Do you often abdicate responsibility to others?
How much do you leave to document "history"?
What do you choose to repair or replace?
Do you keep the form and change the colour?
Do you change the form and keep the colour?
Do you move something from its traditional
position for better effect?
Do you keep old things which impress?
Do you throw them out if they are fake?
Do you work with nature, respecting natural forms
or rhythms?
Do you respect harmony with your location or
surroundings?

**The world will become
peaceful, beautiful and abundant**

IF WE KEEP OUR EYES ON OUR GOAL

If we wish to achieve our goals – and ideally these will be worthy ones – we should have lasting, earnest desire. If desire is short-lived, it will be ineffectual in the final analysis.

We are often used to quick "fixes", immediate solutions and fast food: many never experience a deeper level of "frustration". Therefore, they are sometimes incapable of dealing with the "frustration" which accompanies the highs and lows of long-term projects.

During difficult periods, and whatever our state of action or inaction, we must keep our eyes on the goal. We must not let ourselves become distracted by show or by the inertia of others. We can conceive of ourselves as snowballs rolling, ever collecting up new material, new impulses, new ideas, and growing ever larger. To stand still is to melt in the sun.

This does not mean that we should never take a break. It means that we can use "non-action" time to recover and to make ourselves more amenable to the nuggets of golden inspiration which our unseen guides will place before us in times of stillness, when our ability to listen and receive are the greatest.

**The world will become
peaceful, beautiful and abundant**

**IF WE STOP KNOCKING OUR HEADS
AGAINST A BRICK WALL**

Every NEW YEAR (every NEW DAY is preferable) we are inspired to reflect on the past and to make changes for the future, deciding WHERE TO PLACE OUR ENERGY.

We may realize that we have spent hours doing things which are not actually high priority. We may - on reflection - discover that we are exhausted and "burnt out" because we have put all our effort in a direction which has proved to be unworthy.

Sometimes we find ourselves standing in front of a brick wall. This may be due to impaired health, impeded growth, massive disturbance or stubborn NON-RESPONSE from those we are trying to reach out to and communicate with.

If so, we are invited to CHANGE OUR DIRECTION AND BEHAVIOUR, in order to safeguard our strength and find other ways to actively develop and share our skills.

**The world will become
peaceful, beautiful and abundant**

IF WE PRODUCE OUR OWN ECSTATIC EXPERIENCES WITHOUT DRUGS

Blissful periods of expanded consciousness can be produced through our own effort if we recognise that there is a force greater than ourselves. We connect with this higher wisdom daily, with a view to being connected every moment in the future. We are willing to look at all hindrances which cloud our minds - the unsolved past issues which restrict our forward movement. We decide to clear our minds so that we are able to receive.

Crucially, we are invited to DEVELOP TRUST in the significance of what we see or feel during meditation. It is REAL AND MEANT ESPECIALLY FOR US. We also grow in confidence because we are doing this ENTIRELY BY OURSELVES, requiring no drugs or gurus. Drugs are a crutch, requiring no personal effort. Drugs will LIMIT THE SPIRITUAL EXPERIENCE.

It is our responsibility to see EVERYTHING as an opportunity to grow, teach and improve. If we hold this in our thoughts, mundane days will turn into an adventure. It means that we are always on the lookout. It means that we never lose a chance to assist or comfort someone, never missing the little Divine signs which are placed into our path in order to support our growth.

CHAPTER 4

OUR RESPONSIBILITY TO ACHIEVE
TRUE TRANSPARENCY

**The world will become
peaceful, beautiful and abundant**

IF WE KEEP THINGS SIMPLE

SIMPLE LIVING means that we have much less to wash, clean, organise, replace, repair, conserve, renovate, renew, rearrange, reconstruct, dust, protect, insure or throw out. This means we have more time for health, service to others, shared companionship and creativity. People with many possessions are often preoccupied with worry. It will make a huge difference to let all this go.

SIMPLE COMMUNICATION can be reduced to just three small words: I LOVE YOU, irrespective of what other people might think or say. We should not torment ourselves with imagined phantoms of rejection. It is enough for us to feel the joy of love flowing. We can dance along the street at any time, singing our happiness, peace, confidence and love.

SIMPLE DYING is presently prevented by many traditions and superstitions surrounding this process. It is difficult to conceive of its SIMPLICITY. We move from one existence to the next, like one classroom to the next. It is just the next step on the path. Our beliefs, our sadness, our fears and our expensive traditions make this a VERY DIFFICULT PASSAGE. It is simply another experience towards more joy and knowing. It is as simple as a kiss and goodbye, followed almost immediately by a kiss and hello.

**The world will become
peaceful, beautiful and abundant**

**IF WE UNDERSTAND THAT
EVERY MOMENT IS UNIQUE**

If we look in a mirror, we may think that we always look the same, yet we are continually changing, just as the mirror (which is the world around us, of our own making) changes with us. We would do well to pay attention to these multi-layered perspectives and to realise THE UNIQUE QUALITY OF ANY GIVEN MOMENT.

All moments are unique. We all vary in every second - in our degree of insight, in our mood, in the extent to which unhealed traumas or triggered emotions may colour our view. The scenes around us change as we choose our path and interact with others. Our perceptions are also changing. Is there a "constant" in all this? There is – if we choose it: it is the constant striving towards a sacred goal – also of our own choosing.

If we are afflicted with thoughts such as "He is always so annoying" or "Why do they never realise", we do not recognise this eternal and unique flow. If we use the words ALWAYS or NEVER, we vastly reduce the range of our experience and are forming our future according to preconceived ideas. If we are open for all, all will be open for us, ensured by the cosmic law of balance. The more luggage in the form of pre-conceived ideas and "formulas for success" we carry, the more we will burden ourselves and slow down our journey of adventure.

The world will become
peaceful, beautiful and abundant

IF WE REALISE THAT SOME THINGS ARE THE SAME

If we take a fishbowl full of water, and place it in a lake, we will realise that the water within is THE SAME as the water without. If we place a poverty-stricken woman next to a queen, we may REALISE that their emotional and physical needs, hopes and dreams are THE SAME. If we position a slaughter-house next to a battlefield, we will realise that the bloodshed is THE SAME.

If we point to a clear blue sky, and if someone else points to storm clouds gathering in a different direction, we might do a 180-degree turn and REALISE that they are both part of the SAME SKY.

If we throw waste chemicals into various parts of the earth, we are still polluting the SAME ENVIRONMENT. Moving pollutants "elsewhere" is no guarantee of the purity of our living space. The gaining of such insights is necessary so that our world becomes transparent, as opposed to being too complex and difficult to change.

**The world will become
peaceful, beautiful and abundant**

IF WE EMBRACE TRANSPARENCY AND OPENNESS

Visualisations are a very powerful. Imagine that we are angelic beings, surrounded by light. Our skin is no longer the end of our being, but somewhere in the middle. The surrounding light is our thoughts and energy, and shines to the degree of positive information and creativity we emit. This can be seen immediately by others and

TOUCHES AND MERGES WITH THE LIGHT EMITTED BY OTHERS.

Untoward and harmful thoughts are immediately detected and felt. It is impossible to hide a dark thought, or to hide any intent to cause harm, or to act unjustly.

Fear is instantly recognisable, as well as sadness. Sadness - when it is detected by others - will immediately be addressed and eased.

When the global population increases its level of spirituality, this sort of transparency will revolutionise our society. We will feel and empathise with EVERYTHING. It is the task of all life forms to develop this awareness and to SPREAD LOVE to the best of their ability.

**The world will become
peaceful, beautiful and abundant**

IF WE CONTINUALLY CLEAR THE SPACE WITHIN US

Let us imagine a multitude of miniscule angels entering our heads. Inside, there is a miniature version of our own living space/house. The angels go in and start cleaning up. THEY START TO THROW OUT EVERYTHING WHICH IS OLD OR UGLY OR BROKEN, including old clothes, papers and books we have already read and "digested".

Then they start to polish all the woodwork and brass. They wash, sew and clean. They discover secret corners where hidden secrets lie. They fix bright lights so that everything can be clearly seen.

But this miniscule house is still too dark, so then the angels start peeling back the skin on our scalp, and underneath the skin is a transparent layer which looks like glass. Thus, the outer walls of the living space/house are now fully transparent, and the light radiates strongly.

The message the angels are trying to give us is this:

THROW OUT ALL THE RUBBISH, LEAVE EVERYTHING RELATING TO THE PAST BEHIND, AND ENSURE CLEAN AND EMPTY SPACES SO THAT YOU CAN BETTER BE A VESSEL OF LIGHT.

**The world will become
peaceful, beautiful and abundant**

IF WE CLEAR THE JUNGLE IN OUR MINDS AND IN OUR WORLD

What will we discover in the jungle of our minds? We may discover unrestricted growth of "good" and "bad". We find that the thickets hide atrocities and that the darkness was a convenient cover for heinous criminal acts. We also discover areas of exquisite beauty smothered by overgrowth, which we can detangle and expose for the pleasure of others. We find living creatures in areas where we thought life is impossible. We find the corpses of those who tried to investigate the jungle before us and who did not survive to tell the world about its unpleasant secrets.

The more we enter into the jungle, the deeper will we travel on a physical and also on a mental plane, for the jungle also represents the jungle in our minds which requires radical clearing, resorting, purging and readjustment. Our thoughts are often tangled, confused, dead or throttled, like delicate flowers in the jungle where the undergrowth has grown unimpeded over everything. Will we clear the debris? Will we venture into the "unknown"? Will we follow curiosity although we may come across some devastating new revelation? When we have achieved absolute clarity, we can see which mistakes led to the uncontrolled growth of the jungle, and how this can be avoided in future.

**The world will become
peaceful, beautiful and abundant**

**IF EVERYONE IS AWARE OF THE DECISION-
MAKING PROCESS IN EVERY SECOND**

Even thinking a specific thought is a decision. Every thought is energy which travels. We ourselves are the result of an idea - our parents thought it would be nice to have a child. If we are lucky, that is. Other pairings do not give any thought to the outcome of their sexual activities.

Sometimes we are encouraged to think "positive" thoughts, but this is not enough. If we do not reflect on "negative" situations around us, we are rejecting any responsibility for them. Thus, they cannot be changed.

If we are living in terrible conditions in a war zone, maybe the sight of a daisy (a miracle grown from a tiny seed) will uplift our spirits temporarily, but we still need to deal with our "reality". Having "happy thoughts" will not get to the roots of the problem.

Our present situation is the result of MILLIONS OF DECISIONS - not only our large, life changing decisions, but in every second. How do we decide to react to friends, or to family, or to a stranger? How often do we decide to follow our DIVINE INTUITION? How often do we allow ourselves to be swayed by the interests and opinions of others?

If all this is TRANSPARENT to us, we can change the course of our lives, and the fate of the planet, depending on what principles are guiding our decisions. If we conceive of ourselves as ONE WORLD, united in our efforts to ward off tragedy and self-destruction, then we must align our decisions constantly with the interests of humanity as a whole. This means that our personal "rights" - however valid - take second place to the unity and benefit of the whole.

The world will become
peaceful, beautiful and abundant

IF WE REALISE THAT OUTER VIRUSES ARE A MIRROR OF INNER VIRUSES

At this time of writing, April 2020, when a considerable part of the world is in "quarantine", it is necessary to contemplate WHAT A VIRUS MIRRORS ON THE INNER MENTAL PLANE.

What are the qualities of a virus? It is completely selfish; it moves from one host to another, using all opportunities to spread, without letting others exercise any choice, turning them all into "victims", ruthlessly trying to destroy whatever it encounters, and in such cases, it can only be eradicated through great effort.

It does not affect those who have a good IMMUNE SYSTEM, those who are ALWAYS STRONG AND INDEPENDENT, those who are ALWAYS ALERT TO ANY POSSIBLE DANGER and who TAKE PRECAUTIONS and DETERMINE THEIR OWN DESTINY.

Propaganda which serves a destructive agenda is fashioned to travel like a virus. This can be information which distracts, entertains, or evokes bliss. The "host" wants to continue experiencing this, keeping up a constant "thrill", even if it means self-destruction.

THINKING MODE IS DEACTIVATED, and we slip into automatic, into dependence, into addictions and – because all this is occupying our full attention – we fall into ignorance, oblivious of danger.

Reactivation of THINKING PROCESSES and GROWING OUR MINDS is the answer to raising our mental and spiritual health. If the level of spirituality is raised on this planet, physical health will grow in accordance.

With a high level of spirituality, everything will be COMPLETELY TRANSPARENT. There will be no need to do detailed research, or to try and weed out the truth, BECAUSE EVERYONE WILL BE ONLY TOO HAPPY TO PROVIDE CORRECT, HONEST AND INFORMATIVE DETAILS WHICH SERVE HUMANITY AS A WHOLE.

The world will become
peaceful, beautiful and abundant

IF WE RELEASE NEW TECHNOLOGY
FOR THE BENEFIT OF ALL

The most highly developed technology has so far been reserved for the military, which had the internet long before the general public. We can be sure that if google maps can show us our back gardens, then the military will be able to see what book we are reading when we sit in that garden. One estimate is that military technology is actually 50 years ahead of what is admitted. Technology has been reserved for warring purposes, not for example, for greening the desert.

High levels of technology are not allowed on spiritually low planets, because they would be used for destruction and war. Imagine, for example, a machine which would pulverise anything in sight. This could eradicate huge piles of rubbish which have accumulated on land and in the ocean. It could be used to deal with the sewage system instead of using water. This would clear up pollution and preserve resources. Until earth's inhabitants "grow up" spiritually, however, this technology will not be gifted to us, because we would use it to kill people. It depends on us - and our level of belligerence - as to how soon we will be allowed access to such technology. The prerequisite is a universal desire to preserve peace.

CHAPTER 5

OUR RESPONSIBILITY TO INCREASE OUR PERSONAL SOVEREIGNTY AND INDEPENDENCE

**The world will become
peaceful, beautiful and abundant**

IF WE CONQUER SELF-SABOTAGE

How many times, through a sort of "false modesty" or lack of belief in ourselves have we withdrawn from the scene, denied our capability or refused to see that the ball is in our court? How often have we thought I COULD NEVER DO THAT or I AM NOT THAT SORT OF PERSON or SHE IS SO MUCH BETTER THAN ME.

In some cases, admiration of others is completely justified, yet "feeling small" has nothing to do with others. It results from a lack of confidence in ourselves, and in our own potential to GROW, increasing our skills and therefore our chances with every breath.

Sometimes we deliberately make ourselves "small" and retire from the foreground to make others feel better – so that they are not obscured by our comparative BRILLIANCE. This is called SELF-SABOTAGE. If someone gives us a compliment, do we say "Oh, it's nothing really" or "Oh, I'm sure there are others who can do this just as well" or "Do you really think so?" If so, we are - conscious or subconsciously – on the road to self-sabotage. If someone gives us a compliment and we simply say "thank you", we have overcome this debilitating tendency.

**The world will become
peaceful, beautiful and abundant**

IF WE DECLINE THE SPECIAL OFFERS

Like ants, we scurry around looking for special offers and advantageous purchases. We collect points and bonuses as we go. We partake in "saving schemes", and we simultaneously go on spending sprees. Thus, we line the pockets of those who design the special offers.

We are "well oiled" with incentives and monetary reward. We are seduced by both SALES and DISCOUNTS, or by offers of

TWO FOR THE PRICE OF ONE.

These are all measures of control to make us toe the line. All this keeps us running for the money, perpetuating the system, keeping us off the road of independent thought and action.

Wading through this jungle of offers - involving interest and loans - puts a heavy rucksack on our shoulders. But after a while, carrying this weight feels normal: everyone else is carrying it too, rain or shine, for better or for worse, in sickness and in health.

You will recognise these words, BUT WE ARE NOT MARRIED TO OUR BARGAINS, OUR HOUSES, OUR SYSTEMS, OUR MONEY.

Instead, we are married to the muse of our spiritual progress.

This is our DIVINE COMPANION - THE GODLY ADVISOR WITHIN US WHO IS SO WILLING TO GUIDE US THROUGH EVERYDAY LIFE.

Our divine companions will always listen and assist. They will not bargain for our soul or claim our independence. They will not make us a special roundtrip offer to Paradise. They will not provide a health insurance policy in case we get ill on the way. They will not encourage us to save energy or love for when times get rough, or for a rainy day.

For love should always be spent NOW, given freely and immediately, without question. Accumulating love and locking it in a vault will earn no interest. Our advisors are interested in promulgating our absolute sovereignty.

**The world will become
peaceful, beautiful and abundant**

IF WE DO NOT SUFFOCATE OURSELVES

If we are standing in a full room, we can easily find disguises and aliases. Maybe there are trunks full of fancy dress and masks. Maybe there are people who will put us on a pedestal, or who will condemn us as the scum of the earth. All manner of energies and manipulative currents can influence us in a full, overstuffed room with no windows. Here, the air cannot easily circulate. This means that everything is stagnating and fermenting, permitting no "breath of fresh air".

In a stuffed room, the OLD is venerated and the NEW is defiled. EXPANSION is not possible in a full room, unless one person suffocates another.

Generosity is stifled in the full room. Nothing new can be brought inside, neither can new ideas thrive. The only way to move forward is to squash everyone else into the corners.

The room is called earth. If she is stuffed to bursting point, suffocation is the result. If the floor is covered in debris, it needs sweeping. The windows must be opened and the room filled with light. The roof must be removed.

New seeds must be planted. The room must be transformed into a sacred garden. Her inhabitants must have room to breathe and act independently, acting as the guardians of our precious planet.

**The world will become
peaceful, beautiful and abundant**

IF WE CUT OUT THE MIDDLEMEN

We have created whole classes and sections of society to serve us. We have created individuals called lawyers and organisations to defend us, should we have committed a crime. We have created feel-good gurus to uplift us. We have created insurance companies to protect us, and we have created politicians to ensure our "rights".

We have endowed these people with POWER, thereby abdicating our own. We bow in humility and ignorance to their intricate "knowledge" of the VERY SYSTEM WHICH WE HAVE ALLOWED TO DEVELOP. We have all allowed ourselves to become completely dependent. We CANNOT IMAGINE OUR LIVES ANY OTHER WAY.

It is time to let go of all this. It means letting go of fear. It means representing ourselves instead of letting others take it on. It means protecting our own interests, policing ourselves and taking on responsibilities for others. It means following intuition rather than taking "expert" advice. It means that we are the middlemen and the intersection for all encounters, activities and relationships. It means that we are our own mediator, our own marriage counsellor and our own teacher. Then we will learn what it means to be truly independent.

The world will become
peaceful, beautiful and abundant

IF WE STOP FOLLOWING BLINDLY

Followers rely on someone else - not on their own integrity, discernment and skills. Followers do not make their own decisions, but align with an already determined direction. Followers will question less, falling into complacency, allowing perfidy to grow.

The ideal society consists of LEADERS ONLY. If people are "followers", then this is only temporary in order to learn and to receive inspiration so that they can PAVE THEIR OWN WAY and TEACH THEIR ACQUIRED WISDOM.

How will this make the world more peaceful?

It will prevent one leader, party or nation taking over power and using it to control and destroy. It will prevent the emergence of diverse, belligerent fractions.

It will eliminate the devastating experience that followers might suffer at the realisation that their "guru" is dishonest or guilty of crime.

It will unite us in a stable, peaceful world.

**The world will become
peaceful, beautiful and abundant**

IF WE STOP TAKING PART IN THE THEATRE OF THE ABSURD

People will sometimes seek a diverting night out because they may be inwardly overwhelmed by distressing events. They may visit a cabaret venue where such issues are openly aired.

The audience feels that their deep concerns have been understood. They feel that democracy actually reigns, because the absurdity has been addressed.

They enjoy the confirmation that they are not the only ones who are thinking in a critical way and who recognize the need to take revolutionary action. They sigh with relief. They laugh. All is well. And then they go home.

BUT NOTHING HAS CHANGED

except the dissipation of anxiety. The audience has simply joined in with the ridiculing process, but it has neither offered - nor partaken in - solutions. These are armchair revolutionaries who have been rendered passive, whose passion is watered down by amusement, and who continue to watch the

THEATRE OF THE ABSURD.

**The world will become
peaceful, beautiful and abundant**

IF STAR SEEDS COME OUT OF HIDING

Star seeds are people who have deliberately incarnated on this planet at this specific time. They want to MAKE A DIFFERENCE and TURN A DEPLORABLE SITUATION AROUND. Their work – and any skills they may innately possess and develop – are intended to assist the rebuilding of a new and peaceful society.

However, they have often been prevented from following their intended path. Apart from other obstacles, they erroneously regard themselves as unimportant when they are in fact OLD SOULS who have returned to TEACH AND SHOW THE WAY. Through encountering all sorts of social, financial or political struggles, they have sometimes lost heart and lost their focus, yet it is important for them to "hang on" and develop the ideals with which future development can align.

These people will teach that the thoughts of today will create tomorrow, and that we are always feeding into the manifestation system (instigating cause, and subsequently experiencing effect). They are the pioneers who will push others out of their limited self-created boxes in order to grow and develop their unique potential. May they all COME OUT OF HIDING and benefit all humanity.

The world will be
peaceful, beautiful and abundant

IF WE REALISE THAT THE INSIDE DETERMINES THE OUTSIDE

If we have suffered injury in the past to a certain part of our body, then it may become susceptible to injury again. We are sometimes "prone to injury" in a certain place. All our cells are intelligent and THEY REMEMBER THAT THEY HAVE BEEN HURT BEFORE.

The same thing works on a mental and emotional level. If we have been abandoned by someone, then we are only too ready to weep when we are "abandoned" by the next person.

What can we do about this "cell memory"? We can try and distance ourselves and observe the connections between all interactions, as if we are watching ourselves act on stage in the play of our lives.

If we do this long enough, we will see that everything is a reaction to something else. We will no longer be able to see ourselves as victims. We will become completely sovereign. We will see the consequences of our actions, even if a lengthy period of time has passed between the original cause and the eventual effect. (Time is the element which provides the framework for this learning process). Thus, we will gain wisdom and stability.

**The world will become
peaceful, beautiful and abundant**

IF WE DO NOT WAIT FOR COLLAPSE

Sometimes we may have a hunch that something is not quite right. If so, investigation is necessary to avoid danger. In this, we should trust our intuition. Instead of waiting for the collapse and total chaos, which only few can handle, we should investigate flaws thoroughly. If we make this a habit, then we are more fully prepared for our role as GLOBAL RECONSTRUCTION MANAGERS in all areas.

**The world will become
peaceful, beautiful and abundant**

IF WE REALISE OUR GODLY POWER

The fact that we have godly power is a major realization. It can turn everything UPSIDE DOWN. We know without a doubt that there is a voice inside us which gives DIVINE INSTRUCTIONS. We know that everything which "happens" to us is CREATED BY US. When we realize this, we will go through our WHOLE LIVES again, pinpointing when we felt hurt, abused or neglected. We will be forced to see that we carry partial responsibility. This is a very difficult pill to swallow for those who wish to remain in the role of persecuted victim. But without this realization, we will not be able to access our own power and use it for godly purposes.

CHAPTER 6

OUR DIVINE RESPONSIBILITIES

The world will become
peaceful, beautiful and abundant

IF WE REALISE THAT WE CANNOT GET AWAY WITH ANYTHING

If we turn our heads away from a problem, then later, we will be forced to look. If we scream WOLF, then we can be sure that we will be deceived by the loud cries of others. If we let things "slip", even for a moment, we can expect sudden disruptions to our plans. If we are untruthful, we will be told lies.

Once we have learnt through our own SORRY EXPERIENCE that the law of cause and effect kicks in, whatever the case, then we will assess the consequences of our untruths and criminal acts BEFORE COMMITTING THEM, and we will realize that we cannot get away with them.

We will always be held ACCOUNTABLE in the end, even if we only acknowledge it at the very end of our lives when "passing review".

This may force people to "behave" out of fear of the consequences, yet this is not the aim. The aim is for everyone to VOLUNTARILY ACT IN A WAY WHICH BENEFITS ALL, because they recognize that this is high moral ground.

Many do not yet believe that the universe is run this way, yet its laws are absolute, and our lives will progress with fulfilment if we are in alignment.

**The world will become
peaceful, beautiful and abundant**

IF WE KNOW WHO WE ARE

Possible definitions of ourselves:

"We are all members of a civilised race which has ascended from an animal existence of moral depravity to the heights of a socially conscientious society. We have laws to benefit the less fortunate, and laws to restrict the criminally-minded."

"We have risen from a state of pure survival to a race of savants, artists, writers and technological wizards."

"We are struggling for survival the way our ancestors did before us. We are persecuted and exploited and we see no change on the horizon."

"We have progressed from unorganised chaos and nomadic wandering into a settled and constant way of life, secure within a national and financial system, extended globally".

"We are living in a hiatus, one of many lives, with a specific intent to contribute to the whole picture, of which we are an intricate piece. We are embodiments of our own desire to serve. We are souls, intentionally reincarnating at this time on this particular planet. We act as a catalyst to increase spiritual awareness."

"We are part of the DIVINE WHOLE."

**The world will become
peaceful, beautiful and abundant**

IF WE LIVE THE GREATEST POSSIBLE VERSION OF OURSELVES

Sometimes it is good to take a step back from "everyday life" and remember what we always wanted to do. However, the most important criteria governing our choice is "do unto your neighbour as you would like to be done unto you".

Does our occupation help others? Are we forging a heroic new path to improve conditions on earth? Do we strive to become an expert in some useful field?

If the answer is "no" after such contemplation, we are invited to examine in minute detail

WHY THIS HAS NOT YET COME TO PASS.

Often, we give up our dearest aspirations, thinking that they are "impossible". Sometimes we condemn ourselves for being arrogant and grasping for goals which are "too high".

However, THE SKY IS OUR LIMIT if we work out our visions in great detail and then put them into motion, step by step, determining how we can best use our talents and skills to benefit humankind.

**The world will become
peaceful, beautiful and abundant**

IF PEOPLE DO NOT COMPARE, AND IF THEY TRUST IN THE DIVINE

There is a strong tendency to look for "saviours" outside of ourselves - to revere all sorts of film stars, music icons, religious figures and gurus.

The answers, however, can always be found INSIDE OURSELVES during quiet mediation time. There is a still small voice which - if we allow it and trust it – will provide us with relevant advice.

This may start by us following our "gut reactions" or "intuition", and it may continue by developing into fully fledged conversations with our own divine advisor within. Through experience, our trust in this process will be firmly cemented.

In this way, we will never again be at a loss for what to say or do, because we follow our wise inner lead. Our gaze will be inward, no longer outward. We will trace our own progress with fascination, growing in poise and strength, and we will not feel the need to "follow" anyone else.

We will be completely convinced of our own uniqueness and individuality. This inner guidance will show us what our specific task on earth is, and how best to accomplish it.

**The world will become
peaceful, beautiful and abundant**

IF WE SPREAD THE DIVINE PART OF OURSELVES

When we observe the wonders of nature, we learn that we can take cuttings from certain plants, and they will develop roots under the right conditions. They need no permission or copyright to do so. In the fullness and love which permeates them, they cannot but reproduce constantly, striving to do so in the most perfect way possible.

We can follow this example, spreading the divine part of ourselves, without any thinking, without hesitation, without any thought of loss. We are happy in the knowledge that we are the fount of abundance, that there will always be more from this boundless source, that the energy will always flow, and that the seeds we sow will continue to grow in perfection for eternity.

This is:

BUILDING ANEW TO DIVINE SPECIFICATIONS.

THIS IS RENEWING OUR MISHANDLED, DOWNTRODDEN, AND DESECRATED EARTH.

**The world will become
peaceful, beautiful and abundant**

IF WE CONSTANTLY REMEMBER
THE GOLDEN RULE THAT WE REAP
WHAT WE SOW

Whether beautiful or ugly, violent or peaceful, EVERYTHING HAS SOMETHING TO DO WITH OURSELVES. Our behaviour is the seed, and our surroundings are the fruit of that seed. It is erroneous to say "THAT HAS NOTHING TO DO WITH ME". This attitude is a violent act: we are disassociating ourselves from our fellow humans and collective manifestations. We are leaving others to their "fate", when we actually have the power – through thoughts and actions - to make a difference. We determine the quality of our "effect".

**The world will become
peaceful, beautiful and abundant**

IF WE REALISE THAT WE ARE ONE

When we truly realize this, it will be impossible to even entertain the thought of harming someone else, because we know intrinsically that we are harming ourselves. It will also be impossible to harm the environment, knowing that this ultimately preserves and nourishes us, and is part of our very being. If we extend this to all the universes in space, universal peace is ensured.

**The world will become
peaceful, beautiful and abundant**

IF WE REALISE THAT WE ARE EVERYTHING

All there is, is the verb TO BE, for all are one and there are no spaces in between. We are invited to EXPERIMENT: we can BE another person, country or planet, and we can sense which part of our new body requires healing. The changes we initiate will affect another plane. We can BE a new and different version of ourselves, trying on the skin of another. We can extend our awareness and heal a part of ourselves by healing a part of another.

Can you see where this is heading? We are the drop of water in a polluted ocean. We are a genetically manipulated seed planted in a field which has been doused with artificial fertiliser. We are a small tender plant strangled by rampant weeds. We are a million stars in a far-flung galaxy. If we can take on these roles, we will ask WHY and search for solutions. If we are in polluted water, we will seek METHODS OF PURIFICATION. If we are a genetically manipulated seed, we will seek to REVERSE ADVERSE PROGRAMING. If we are planted in contaminated soil, we will seek METHODS TO REGNERATE NATURALLY. If we are strangled by weeds, we will seek to CLEAR THE MENTAL JUNGLE. And if we are a million stars, we will be encouraged to LIVE OUR INFINITE POTENTIAL AND SPREAD ETHEREAL LIGHT ETERNALLY.

**The world will become
peaceful, beautiful and abundant**

IF THE WHOLE LANDSCAPE IS SURVEYED

If we decide to look intensely in one direction only, or if we consider only one part of the body while attempting to make a diagnosis of the whole, we are missing the greater picture, and this can lead to erroneous decisions.

While it can also be beneficial to have "experts" in every field, rigid division between subjects can encourage "disconnect" and a distorted view, just as intense involvement in any group fighting for rights may prevent understanding and even encourage conflict with other groups.

Surveying "the whole landscape" - including the ants on the ground, the mountains on the horizon and the deepest of oceans - encourages a feeling of balance, and prevents error and extremism.

Concentrating on a narrow "field" may be beneficial for a short while, but it is debilitating in the long run if there is no opportunity to stop, widen our horizon, and experience the exhilaration of an OPEN LANDSCAPE WHICH STRETCHES AS FAR AS THE EYE CAN SEE, AND BEYOND.

It is this "beyond" in our imagination, as opposed to what we can presently actually see, which inspires us to recognise that there is SO MUCH MORE WE CAN EXPERIENCE IN THE FUTURE.

**The world will become
peaceful, beautiful and abundant**

IF WE HOLD THE WHOLE SPECTRUM IN OUR MINDS DURING SIMPLE PROCESSES

We might be standing under the shower, bleary-eyed, thinking that the water might wake us up. We adjust the temperature, first letting the warm water (if we have that luxury at all) run till it is boiling hot, and then we add cold water until it is EXACTLY THE RIGHT TEMPERATURE. All the time we are assessing the temperature of the water to see if it is RIGHT FOR US.

But there are other perspectives which we COULD carry in our mind simultaneously, for example where has the water come from, how often has it been processed or cleaned? What information is it carrying? What effect does this information have on us? Where does the water go?

What information are WE feeding into the water - love or aggression? Whatever the quality, it will be circulated to others once we have finished showering, and it will ultimately return to ourselves (through the recycling of water on our earth) at a later date.

We can practice holding the whole spectrum in our minds during simple processes, adding love to the mix.

**The world will become
peaceful, beautiful and abundant**

IF WE ARE ALWAYS IN THE FLOW

If we sit in a quagmire of stagnation, whether in our personal or vocational life, we may be fairly numbed to the idea that everything (YES, EVERYTHING) could get into swing, like an enormous river sweeping blockages away.

Some people are resigned, some are complacent, some are in denial of this possibility. Others just feel helpless and therefore cannot find any strength in themselves to go into action, let alone remove others who stand in their way.

To be in the flow is to

RIDE ON THE EDGE OF HISTORY.

It means that we are continually breathless with excitement. It means that we laugh (and in many cases, also to cry) incessantly so that our emotions are given a thorough wash and release.

We need courage to face and defeat obstacles, which are often of our own making. Thus can we unburden ourselves and step forward, leaving burdensome debris behind us.

**The world will become
peaceful, beautiful and abundant**

IF WE CAN STOP FOCUSSING ON TIME

Rather than measuring time, we can measure intensity. We often divide our lives into parcels of time. If we think in a purely linear manner, we miss the point, or we miss the process.

Intensity is the yardstick, if we want to assess whether we are really ALIVE and following our vocation.

Time is but an instrument allowing us to learn and experience - not a unit whereby the quality of "work", "friendships" or "relationships" can be measured.

True friendships are TIMELESS in the sense that it does not matter how much time lies between two intense encounters.

Focus on time is often unhealthy and debilitating. We may be deterred, for example, from launching into a huge project because we worry about the

LONG TIME IT WILL TAKE.

Our journey (whether successful or not) may be just as interesting as our goal. We do not need to wait, or to look for a fair wind. Our decisions can be instant and in every moment. This is the intensity we lack and which will propel forward progress.

**The world will become
peaceful, beautiful and abundant**

IF WE LOOK INSIDE FOR THE ANSWERS

If we always think we are innocent, and look for the "culprit", we are playing the BLAME GAME. We might feel genuinely aggrieved, and we may feel that it is perfectly within our rights to blame and attack others for our misfortunes. On one level, there is some truth in this, as we may be born into countries, societies or families which do not have our wellbeing at heart.

However, on another level, we are always being presented with the next learning experience. Whether consciously or subconsciously, we have specifically chosen our location and circumstances before birth. The worse the situation, the steeper the learning curve, and the more progress we achieve.

Some people say LOOK DOCTOR (or politician, guru, pope or god), I'VE GOT THIS ILLNESS. NO IDEA WHY, JUST GIVE ME A PILL. These people do not want to look at themselves or accept responsibility for their present state. They present themselves as VICTIMS. If we self-reflect, and if we "go within" for answers instead of rushing around to consult "experts", we develop stability and trust in the process, and so, when any problem arises, we do not need anyone to come along and save us. Indeed, WE SAVE OURSELVES.

**The world will become
peaceful, beautiful and abundant**

IF WE CHOOSE LIGHT OVER DARK

Pressure accumulates due to the conflict between light and dark, between altruism and selfishness, between love and fear, between exposure and secrets. Especially at the end of cosmic cycles, these pressures will become acute. Previously, we may have been able to look away, or concentrate on something different, or enjoy something unrelated. At the closure of a cycle, increasing cosmic energies, especially gamma rays, force us to choose. There is no more "sitting on the fence".

As a result, we may feel like we are shining a torch into a dark, cavernous storage room. We will suddenly see an array of forgotten objects. This may be a shock to our systems. We will be forced to reintegrate these hidden "surprises" into our consciousness, and adjust our thinking. We will wonder HOW DID THESE OBJECTS GET THERE and DID I EVEN KNOW THAT THIS ROOM EXISTED? For those who answer NO, this will be a devastating experience. For others, it will be the realisation of their worst fears.

For others, it will be the confirmation of their suspicions or the proof of their researches. For others, who have been crouching in the dark recesses of the room for years, it will be the sudden demise of their reputations and full exposure of their negative intent. How can all this be prevented? The answer is that we must fill the room with "light" - again and again and again – so that the dark cannot cover anything up.

**The world will become
peaceful, beautiful and abundant**

IF WE CHOOSE TO LOSE IN ORDER TO WIN

Doing a job thoroughly may seem straightforward, but this is because we have a very subjective view or fixed ideas. In truth, no task is "straightforward". If it was, we would not evolve, we would not grow as a result, and this is why challenging tasks are placed in our path.

If something is very easily achieved, it has not "stretched" us to the limit. It has not spurred us on to perfection.

Sometimes it is necessary to give up cherished parts of a plan, or cherished words of a text, or cherished friends on a particular road of life. This may cause feelings of pain or loss. However, we must sometimes do so in order to develop new and better plans, in order to improve the quality of a text, or in order to part ways temporarily so that they can more strongly re-join at a later date.

Thus, we choose to lose in order to win. In this way, we are doing our jobs thoroughly.

**The world will become
peaceful, beautiful and abundant**

IF WE EXPAND OUR IDEA OF GOD

What does it feel like to live under centuries of oppression, cruelty and exploitation? Our earth has been blanketed in "heaviness" for a long time. What shall we do? To whom shall we turn for help? What is GOD? An angry person sitting on a cloud, seeking revenge and sitting in judgement of everything which happens on earth? Can this be a source of inspiration and assistance?

GOD is the DIVINE COMPASS WITHIN US, as well as the UNIVERSAL CONSCIOUSNESS WHICH PERMEATES ALL OF CREATION. If we develop complete trust in this "inner compass", we will sail blissfully through perfectly clear waters, with complete poise and confidence in our abilities, serene and content, spreading light on our way to our chosen destination.

**The world will become
peaceful, beautiful and abundant**

IF WE EMBRACE THE ABSOLUTE

What would happen if we no longer take important things "lightly?" What if we step courageously out of our hiding places? What if we never knowingly abuse? What if we never accept the "lesser way"?

What if we always insist on quality? What if we co-operate constantly? What if we never sacrifice integrity in our daily lives?

What if we never let ego influence our decisions? What if we are always impeccably honest? What if we always give our all?

It is up to us to decide WHAT DEGREE OF COMMITMENT and WHAT ASPECTS OF THE ABSOLUTE we choose to embrace, but we can be sure that the higher it is, the more peaceful, beautiful and abundant the world will become.

CHAPTER 7

OUR RESPONSIBILITIES IN
RELATIONSHIPS

**The world will become
peaceful, beautiful and abundant**

IF MAN AND WOMAN TRULY COMPLEMENT AND RESPECT EACH OTHER

Throughout millennia, women have been considered inferior, used for hard menial work and "sex satisfaction". All these experiences are recorded in the earth's genetic mind as a program which influences the next generation. It is our collective task to REWRITE these programs through our PRESENT BEHAVIOUR.

The "divide" between men and women is one of the most devastating and deeply ingrained characteristics of our world. Many women have fought, rightly, for justice; many have rejected masculinity outright, and fight militantly, causing separation.

What is required here is BALANCE and mutual respect, not insisting on "equality" but on OUR RECOGNITION OF UNIQUENESS and in appreciation of ALL THAT WHICH MAKES EACH SEX SPECIAL. Each sex has developed its own "strategies" to deal with their disadvantages, or to assure their advantages. These have also caused much grief. Asking forgiveness of men, in the name of all women, and asking forgiveness of women, in the name of all men, is an essential step. In this way, the age-long rift between man and woman will have a chance to heal.

**The world will become
peaceful, beautiful and abundant**

IF WE TRANSITION FROM I MATTER
TO WE MATTER

Many people on this planet have risen through difficult circumstances, or have suffered due to prevailing low frequency conditions or structures.

They have come through with strength, convinced of the fact – whatever anyone else might think or say – that THEY MATTER, irrespective of origin, or any other factor.

They and we do matter, and the thought of this will carry us far along a successful path. The danger of this, however, is that this path is ours alone.

If we are convinced that we matter MORE THAN OTHERS, we will propel division, fuel violence and demonstrate arrogance.

One of the most important transition of our times is to take up the fight for the RIGHTS OF ALL, transitioning from I MATTER to WE MATTER.

The world will become
peaceful, beautiful and abundant

IF WE LOVE CHILDREN UNCONDITIONALLY
FROM THE VERY MOMENT OF CONCEPTION

Love energy is extremely powerful. If a woman and her expected child are constantly loved throughout pregnancy and beyond, this brings extra stability to all. The developing baby is capable of feeling and hearing. Fatherhood and motherhood does not begin at birth, but before conception. For this to be achieved, there can be no "one night stands", for these might result in a "surprise" or not previously considered pregnancy. This is possible if everyone has reached a high level of spirituality, including SELF-CONTROL. All this is possible if one LOVES ENOUGH. What does this really mean? It means that everyone feels so responsible for everyone else, including unborn children, that the idea of risking conception before actually TALKING TO and INVITING a particular soul to be part of their family IS UNTHINKABLE. This invitation takes place BEFORE CONCEPTION. Those who wish to become parents will take PARENT COURSES in order to best prepare - mentally, physically and spiritually - BEFORE CONCEPTION. Thus will a generation of children be raised who have grown up in stable, peaceful and loving families. Those who are born into circumstances where the spiritual vibration is high, will have an excellent head start on their own spiritual journey.

**The world will become
peaceful, abundant and beautiful**

IF WE PAY ATTENTION TO THE
REQUESTS OF OTHERS

How many times do we actually MISS THE POINT of what someone is trying to tell us, simply because we are engrossed in our own affairs? Sometimes we interrupt as soon as we recognize something familiar. We inject our own experience, forcing the dialogue to go off at a tangent. Sometimes, our empathy is not deep enough to TAKE SOMEONE SERIOUSLY. If someone makes a small request, which is easy to fulfill, DO WE BOTHER TO DO IT? And why is it THAT WE CANNOT BE BOTHERED?

The word BOTHER means that we consider the person making the request as someone who is ENCROACHING UPON OUR OWN SPACE and TAKING UP OUR TIME. This ensues from the idea that we NEVER HAVE ENOUGH TIME, so we try and protect our boundaries and only give in to that which seems to be EXTREMELY IMPORTANT.

If, however, we consider small requests as big important requests, cosmic law will kick in, ensuring that our own requests will be fulfilled with alacrity, especially when they mean a lot to us. REAL LISTENING - and trying to find out how someone ticks and what is valuable to them - is a way of increasing understanding, communication and - ultimately - PEACE.

**The world will become
peaceful, beautiful and abundant**

IF WE ARE PREPARED TO TAKE TIME TO REPAIR OUR RELATIONSHIPS

Many relationships suffer due to "stress", lack of time and lack of communication. The following very valuable exercise, which only takes 10 minutes of our day, is capable of saving marriages.

Partner A says nothing, and just listens. Partner B has 5 minutes to talk about anything they want to, without interruption. The sentences should begin with "I" or "I feel". The word "you" is to be avoided. This is about expressing personal feelings, not about accusing others. If there is a break, or silence, then partners should sit out the 5-minute slot in silence.

Then, partner B says nothing and just listens. Partner A now has 5 minutes to express their feelings, in the same manner as above.

When this 10-minute ritual is over, both partners go off and do something by themselves. They do not talk to each other for the next half an hour.

This allows new "mental spaces" to open up, resulting in increased understanding, acceptance and compassion.

**The world will become
peaceful, beautiful and abundant**

IF WE PEER INTO EACH OTHER'S SOULS

Can we conceive of a world where all material needs are met, and where the eyes of everyone we meet rest on our faces alone?

All else – our clothes, surroundings or status – will be peripheral. Other people will not be interested in the way we officially present ourselves to the outside world. They will look deep into our soul and listen to the tune which is being played within.

THE DIVINE IS CONSTANTLY PEERING INTO OUR SOUL. It is not distracted by outward facades or shows. It loves UNCONDITIONALLY. Nothing can make the DIVINE or GOD or CREATION turn away from us. No petty difference or momentary failure to pay attention will draw it away from us.

WE ARE THE CONSTANT FOCUS OF THIS CONSTANT LOVE. No force is powerful enough to PREVENT THIS LOVING EMBRACE.

CHAPTER 8

OUR SOCIAL
RESPONSIBILITIES

**The world will become
peaceful, beautiful and abundant**

IF EVERYONE WORKS

The universal desire to serve our fellow humans is essential to peace.

For millennia, our main incentive has been to serve ourselves.

In a world where everyone regards others with benevolence, everyone will be on the receiving end of benevolence.

Society, or governments, presently support large classes of "unemployed". In some cases, support is justified. In others, it is not.

If everyone who is capable of work feels a constant inner urge to contribute to society, the words "work", "leisure", "employed" and "unemployed" will gradually lose their meaning. Everyone will enjoy fulfilment as a result of constant service to others.

As the level of spirituality rises, no one will feel justified in receiving "benefits" while doing nothing. Service to others, rather than service to an organization or affiliation or political party, will be the most highly regarded of all offices.

**The world will become
peaceful, beautiful and abundant**

IF WE ARE UNDIVIDED IN OUR LOYALTIES

Life on earth requires constant "working together". However, there are so many different personalities and sets of behaviours represented on our planet which impede progress:

Some people push and pull, convinced that they know "how things should be", although they do not have the adequate technical knowledge or spiritual sensitivity to achieve perfect execution. Some people know a great deal, but they are too lazy to apply it, or too damaged to voice it. Some people are experts at oversight but are not expert in any one category. Some people are easily unbalanced. Some are excellent mediators, but this sometimes prevents necessary discussion and stifles conflicts which require expression. There are those who work silently and independently behind the scenes but who realise later that they have been rigidly following a direction which does not benefit the majority. Some make unilateral decisions as a result of fear or ego, without informing others. Some do not take into account the far-reaching effects of their choices on others.

Some people work constantly in the belief that this is their duty, only to collapse from overwork and to accuse others of sloth. Some manipulate others into doing what they don't want to do themselves, using compliments and flattery. There are those who frequently show gratitude to their fellow workers through words of genuine praise, but they fail to value their own work. There are those who feel the pressure quickly and who resort to frequent breaks to feed their various addictions.

There are those who cannot deviate from their own routine under any circumstances. Some people appear to have integrity, but they simply watch the struggle of their fellows, once their own allotted work is done. There are those who are born leaders but who take on too much responsibility. There are those who are convinced of their mediocrity and insignificance, who allow themselves to be dominated.

There are perfectionists who cannot delegate, or who draw out processes unnecessarily, causing delays for others. There are those who put in consistent effort and make themselves martyrs. There are those who make promises and commitments which they do not keep. There are those who leave in exasperation because sche-dules and assignments are changed without their consultation.

How is it possible to unite all these diverse personalities? Some of them are communicative. Some are loners. Some are eager for human contact. Some lead, and some follow. How can they be brought together to co-ordinate a huge project so that it succeeds in scope, quality and purpose?

It is important that we constantly self-reflect, assessing our behaviour. It is important that we recognize Divinity in all other human beings. Ideally, at the end of every working day, people will sit together respectfully and talk, not boasting about what they have done, but telling each other what they have learnt and how they could improve.

**The world will become
peaceful, beautiful and abundant**

IF WE GIVE PRAISE WHERE PRAISE IS DUE

It is an interesting experiment to count how many times we praise someone or say "thank you" in the course of a day. How many times do we say THANK YOU and really mean it?

If we are parents, we instinctively praise our children for their progress. We clap with excitement at their very first step, and we are delighted by each new word our child manages to speak.

The world would change if we could apply this deep love and understanding to strangers passing by, as well as close friends and family.

This does not mean endorsing everything which comes along, but outwardly expressing sincere appreciation where it is due.

**The world will become
peaceful, beautiful and abundant**

IF EDUCATION IS REPLACED BY EDUCATING

The phrase "to be given an education" suggests that students simply sit in classes and are GIVEN knowledge. "Interaction" with the educator may be 30 to 1. This leaves students in a passive stance.

Even if their thirst for learning is aroused, they do not have much opportunity to voice this as individuals. They are only one in a crowd of faces, in a limited period of time. Most lessons are cut off after 40 minutes, preventing full immersion in any one subject.

WHAT IF EVERYONE IS AN EDUCATOR?

Each student will learn about a certain topic

IN ORDER TO TEACH IT - ONE TO ONE - TO ANOTHER STUDENT.

There will be no time limits involved. The learning student will receive full attention, and the teaching student will consolidate their own knowledge, and increase their self-confidence and independence.

This facilitates rapid, effective and joyful learning.

**The world will become
peaceful, beautiful and abundant**

**IF THE NEXT GENERATION IS EDUCATED BY
A REVISED CURRICULUM**

The school system must be revolutionised,
introducing completely new subjects of study:

COMMUNICATION, SPIRITUAL LIVING,
CONFLICT RESOLUTION, SELF-
IMPROVEMENT, RELATIONSHIPS, DANCING /
SINGING / MUSIC-MAKING, GROWING FOOD
and PROTECTING THE ENVIRONMENT.

Teamwork will receive special attention, as well as
discussions on LOVE and what that actually means
in daily life. There will also be a special focus on
CREATIVITY: resilient citizens are CREATIVE
AND FLEXIBLE ONES.

Students will be encouraged to develop their skills
- including very practical skills - so that they are well
equipped for some sort of trade, and in addition
they will be encouraged to pursue their own specific
interests with a view to

FULFILLING THEMSELVES

but also in consideration of

IMPROVING THE LIVES OF OTHERS.

**The world will become
peaceful, beautiful and abundant**

IF WE SHOW TOTAL COMMITMENT TO THE WELFARE OF OTHERS

If we consider the military structures and striking capabilities of global powers, it may be difficult to see how we personally support and enable them. However, all soldiers are clothed, fed and paid. Weapons are made, transported, made operational and deployed. This is not personally conducted by any specific "elite". The whole military structure is SUPPORTED by those who conform and obey. We make these compromises for the love of money (which has become our idol). Our conforming behaviour enables others to be destroyed.

Occasional neighbourly friendliness will not save us from any emotional turmoil which may be festering below. A pleasant "hello" to our neighbours across the fence may be all very well, but it does not spell out our

TOTAL COMMITMENT TO THE WELFARE OF OTHERS, IRRESPECTIVE OF THEIR COUNTRY. IT IS THIS UNCOMPROMISING COMMITMENT WHICH IS THE PRE-REQUISITE FOR PEACE ON THIS PLANET.

**The world will become
peaceful, beautiful and abundant**

**IF PEOPLE REALISE THAT
CURING THEMSELVES IS
SIMULTANEOUSLY CURING OTHERS**

This happens on a mental level, illustrated by the experience of one doctor in charge of a mental asylum. He practiced the Hawaiian method of forgiveness, Ho'oponopono. (based on the principles of "I'm sorry, please forgive me, thank you, I love you"). The doctor did not visit his patients. Instead, he went into meditation and asked which negative aspects of his own behaviour corresponded with which patient. He then improved his own behaviour, and the patients improved also. As a result, all patients were cured.

Family constellation sessions also show how one person's change affects the entire morphogenetic field. If one person in a family CHANGES THEIR ATTITUDE OR BEHAVIOUR, then one cog in the system starts to work in a different way, forcing all the other cogs to adapt and CHANGE IN THEIR TURN. This works ON ALL LEVELS, illustrated well by the saying "If a butterfly flaps its wings, it will cause a storm on the other side of the world". Our every word and movement has an EFFECT. It is our choice whether to use our words and actions for positive or negative purposes. We can choose behaviour which has a beneficial effect on the GLOBAL FAMILY.

**The world will become
peaceful, beautiful and abundant**

**IF EVERYONE BECOMES A
PILLAR OF SOCIETY**

What is a pillar of society?

Someone who is in the public eye

Someone who does not choose to retire passively
into the shadows

Someone who is always considering the
general good

Someone who puts their own needs "on hold"

Someone who is dedicated to improving all
aspects of life for others and for themselves

Someone who upholds moral values

Someone who acts as a father/mother figure
for those in distress

Someone who tries to sort out disagreements
and uphold the peace

Someone who is always ready to listen to
complaints

Someone who is always prepared to find the
best solution

Someone who recognizes their own flaws
and addresses them

Someone who always keeps an eye on the disadvantaged

Someone who is entirely approachable for everyone

**The world will become
peaceful, beautiful and abundant**

IF WE ALL COMMIT TO A FORM OF PUBLIC SERVICE

On planets which are more spiritually advanced than ours (AND MANY OF THEM ARE), it is the greatest honour to be awarded a position as a "public servant". Only those who have great integrity and humility are chosen for this service. These are the most respected officials.

On earth at the present time (in 2020), many people work in the field of public service. Some do so out of complete conviction, others less so. Money still dominates most decisions.

Ideally, everyone should reflect on how they can contribute to their community, whether this is officially part of their "normal job" or not. Selfishness will eventually be replaced by altruism.

**The world will become
peaceful, beautiful and abundant**

IF RISKS ARE ELIMINATED
AND COSTS AVOIDED

Sometimes we may harbour a worthy goal. At the same time, the direction and dedication required to achieve it may be so great and "one-sided" that the COST is too much for us.

The COST is not only financial expenditure but also the cost of HUMAN LIVES (for example the lives lost in the building of huge dams).

The cost is also:

DAMAGE TO THE ENVIRONMENT

such as contamination by nuclear waste. In the past, for example, nuclear waste has been stored in oceans in containers destined to last only fifty years – resulting in yet more contamination later.

Why would anyone choose this sort of container? And why would anyone in their right mind build a nuclear facility on a known fault line?

There are only two explanations for this sort of behaviour. The first is ignorance and stupidity. The second is that RISKS WERE CALCULATED AND HAVE DELIBERATELY BEEN TAKEN.

**The world will become
peaceful, beautiful and abundant**

IF WE DEVELOP PERFECT SYNCHRONICITY

Swarms of birds will fly together AS ONE, in perfect synchronicity. As they fly, they collect more and more members of the group, and the newcomers are in alignment with the rest. They fly together in one direction in general consensus. This is something to be imitated by humankind. No long discussions, but clear and precise intuitive decisions on the direction to be taken, and then immediate lift-off.

There will be no need for memos and no need to take issues to higher authorities to be sanctioned

BECAUSE EVERYONE WILL BE THEIR OWN HIGHEST AUTHORITY, ACTING WITH ONE HUNDRED PERCENT RESPONSIBILITY IN THE BEST INTERESTS OF ALL.

Holding to this principle will ensure that the direction taken will bear good fruit. It will iron out any confusion or opposing views. Everyone will wish to benefit the majority. Everyone will recognise that their own personal needs are sometimes not as important as the whole. This is not to say that basic rights and legitimate desires are to be surrendered, but that ego-related actions and irresponsible, squandering tendencies

NEVER ARISE.

**The world will become
peaceful, beautiful and abundant**

IF WE EMULATE BEES

Bees fly constantly from one flower to another. If a flower is unable to give nectar, BEES DO NOT SHOUT AND SCREAM OR INSIST ON ANOTHER FLOWER PROVIDING IT. They just move on.

NEITHER WILL BEES HOARD NECTAR IN HIDDEN PLACES OUT OF FEAR THAT THERE MAY, ONE DAY, NOT BE ENOUGH.

Bees continue without pausing, collecting what they can FOR THE GOOD OF THE COLLECTIVE.

There is no complaining. There is no envy. There is no ego. There is no delight in having collected more nectar than another bee. There is no difference in outward attire to suggest that one bee has gathered more than the next. There is no exploitation. There is no propaganda.

There are no advertisements put out by the flowers saying COME TO ME BECAUSE MY NECTAR TASTES THE BEST AND MAKES YOU MORE ATTRACTIVE TO OTHER BEES. There are no signs saying THESE FLOWERS ARE RESERVED FOR QUEEN BEES ONLY.

There are no contracts which say IF YOU
RETRIEVE THIS AMOUNT OF NECTAR, YOU
RECEIVE MORE ADVANTAGES.

Bees do not force their way into a bud which is not
already open. They do not destroy the plant in the
process. They do not say OH, NOW IT IS THE
WEEKEND. I CAN'T WORK TODAY.

They do not clock in to work. No one needs to check
whether they have completed their task. They do so
automatically, as this is their contribution. They do
not get paid.

They enjoy abundance and give abundantly. They
have no punishing or judicial systems. They are
self-regulatory.

Bees do not cry or make petulant noises when they
do not find what they want the first time around.
They patiently keep going.

They are not angry with other bees for getting to the
nectar first. They bear no grudges.

They are focussed on the communal goal. They act
according to instinct, for the common good. They
are not selfish. They have a strong loyalty to
"family" and to ONENESS.

**The world will become
peaceful, beautiful and abundant**

IF WE TREAT ANIMALS
AS WE TREAT OURSELVES

Why are wild animals aggressive? Do they have a reason? Their fear arises from the fact that they have been exploited and hunted for millennia. Their fear of violent humans is firmly planted in the genetic mind of the earth. This fear is documented in an "instruction file" which is "downloaded" by animals. We can rewrite the content of such files by "writing" new instructions. This is accomplished by replacing our violent behaviour with LOVE. Humans engage better if they are happy and well. The same is true of animals. They must be loved and well treated.

The great demand for meat still determines and dominates landscapes. Huge tracts of land and amounts of water are dedicated to the production of cattle. Vast areas are devoted to growing maize as pig fodder. But for most people, eating meat is not essential to health. On the contrary, it requires hours of digestion, it inserts unhealthy "medicines" and substances into our bodies, and it requires the death of a living being. New technologies are being developed which can "grow" meat without involving animals. This is the future, a largely vegetarian world where humans treat animals with kindness.

**The world will become
peaceful, beautiful and abundant**

IF EVERYONE JOINS A CHOIR

The idea that someone cannot sing is erroneous. We all have an instrument called a VOICE, and like so many other endowments and situations, the question is "Do we make use of it?"

Many children, who have been told in childhood or at school that they have a "terrible voice", are convinced for the rest of their lives that this avenue is closed to them. Yet it is always open.

Singing, like dancing and being creative in an expressive way, is not only a joy but a great teacher. To sing in a choir is peace in motion, since all voices adjust to form ONE BEAUTIFUL SOUND, just as all people on earth will adjust to form ONE PEACEFUL WORLD IN HARMONY.

Egotism has no place in choirs and orchestras. Their members hold back or change for the sake of the whole. We will learn to support each other, perform together and celebrate together. May the whole world become a choir.

**The world will become
peaceful, beautiful and abundant**

IF WE REWRITE EARTH'S GENETIC MIND

We can actually compare the mind of the earth to a computer. Every thought, word and action which has taken place on our earth, right from the very beginning, is stored in the earth's genetic mind on millions of "files". These constitute a huge pool of knowledge which can be accessed by those in search of information. For example, information is available for all animals to "download". This is where they get "instincts" from.

Human beings also download knowledge, yet much of the available information consists of regressive, corrupt and violent behaviour – the result of many devastating wars which have taken place on the planet. These files and programmes are influencing everyone adversely, and they need to be

REWRITTEN.

The present inhabitants of earth can do this by behaving in a different way, by allowing their actions to be compassed by love and compassion. These new "programmes" will similarly be written into earth's mind and become "available" to future generations, generating new, peaceful behaviours.

**The world will become
peaceful, beautiful and abundant**

IF WE CONTROL OUR POPULATION AND IMPROVE OUR GENETICS

A considerable percentage of our populations are afflicted in some way by hereditary disease or ailment. Although they can have happy and fulfilling lives, sometimes turning into inspirational figures, this is not an optimal situation. The quality of our "genetic material" is generally on the decrease. How can these limitations be reduced, or even avoided?

Leading edge medical research and technology will, when released and fully available, be able to make a difference in certain cases. But what about the other cases? Would a highly spiritual person with an extremely strong sense of personal and global responsibility, who KNOWS that they carry a defective gene or hereditary illness, make a deliberate and conscious decision to have a child?

This, initially, may seem like "giving up on one's rights", but if CHOSEN by the individual, as a way of improving the "genetic pool", then that is not their sacrifice but their deliberate contribution, freely given. When everyone develops this level of conscience, everyone in the future will have the blueprint for a perfectly working body.

Exploding population on earth has overburdened our planet and exploited her resources. If there is over-population, she will develop some strategy to throw us off. We must therefore "hold back" to benefit earth and humanity as a whole.

CHAPTER 9

OUR CULTURAL
RESPONSIBILITIES

The world will become
peaceful, beautiful and abundant
IF MUSIC IS CONTINUALLY USED
TO UPLIFT, NURTURE AND COMFORT

Music, the language that everyone understands, is the greatest tool to uplift the soul. It can also be used to destroy, manipulate and desensitize, under laid by negative tracks which cannot be heard by the ear but which influence the subconscious. Making music together in orchestras or choirs, experiencing synergy effects as well as hearing the unique quality of every human voice, benefits individuals on their learning journey and serves as excellent quality entertainment for communities.

The world will become
peaceful, beautiful and abundant
IF MORE FORMS ARE ROUND

A round conference table allows all participants to see all other participants. Everyone is included. There is no sense of hierarchy. If friends or family gather round a circular table, the effect is the same. If chairs face off towards each other, they invite conversation and interaction. If they are placed so direct eye contact is impossible, they will promote loneliness. Round houses and round villages (perhaps surrounded by a stream or circular road) have a feeling of cosiness and togetherness. And all circles have a centre, a focal point, a place to gather and socialize.

**The world will become
peaceful, beautiful and abundant
IF WE BECOME AWARE OF THE
POWER OF COLOUR**

Colours can be used for positive or negative effect. Neon pink has a violent effect, and it has been used extensively in toys for girls. Blue is calming, and has been used extensively in toys for boys.

If we do some historical research, we discover that this was once the other way around. It has been changed on purpose to encourage aggression in girls and meekness in boys.

The myriad greens of nature and the blue sky have a soothing effect. Those who live in urban areas may not have so much exposure to this. Blue or green painted walls will help. Yellow walls uplift and increase enthusiasm. If we wish to experiment, we can decide to paint layer upon layer of thin yellow watercolour. If we do this for an hour, it will have an uplifting effect.

We are always subconsciously influenced by our environment. We can develop our awareness: What colours surround us? Are our rooms drab and sterile? Are they ordered or chaotic? All this will influence our mood. If we all develop more sensitivity, we will create buildings, areas and gardens which uplift our spirits continuously.

**The world will become
peaceful, beautiful and abundant**

IF SPORT REGAINS ITS TRUE SIGNIFICANCE

"Sport is a peripheral activity, undertaken in free time in order to improve health". This is the sort of general statement which does very little to cover this vast subject: its benefits are not confined to the physical realm.

Practicing certain sports means practicing balance and alacrity of response. Sport makes use of energy to create a synergy affect. It shows that determined practice can result in strong self-discipline, confidence and self-improvement. It fosters teamwork, cooperation and feelings of unity. It increases concentration and focus. It encourages striving for perfection.

If not taken to extremes, sport improves health. It shows us which parts of our physical bodies are not in 100% working order.

As many sports take place out of doors, this puts us in direct contact with nature and the elements. We experience a quickening of all systems when we are "out of breath". We experience how we cope with stress. Sport can remove us from daily routines, placing us squarely into the NOW. It can exhilarate us, give us insights, and most of all it can provide us with company and companionship.

**The world will become
peaceful, beautiful and abundant**

IF WE CULTIVATE AND CELEBRATE BEAUTY IN THE ARTS

The current celebration of a grotesque culture of ugliness and destruction in the arts is another of the absurdities which we must reverse. Cool, sterile interiors will not enliven our mood. Depiction of violent scenes or subject matter in art will not elevate the spirit. Unaesthetic performances will not inspire. Discordant and repetitive music will not sooth. Wearing ragged clothing on skin which has been excessively tattooed and pierced will not improve our sense of well-being. At the moment, perversion in art is applauded, self-harm in fashion and other areas is encouraged, and violence and killing in films (as well as in real life) proliferates. This is all called "cool".

To achieve the opposite of "cool" is to encourage that which WARMS AND DELIGHTS THE HEART. Art has a strong mission: the first stage of art is representing a subject or theme by copying. The next stage is representing a subject or theme in one's own style, demonstrating uniqueness. The next stage is to use the subject matter to send an important message. And the last stage, which amounts to a mission, is to use all forms of art and performance as an instrument of SPIRITUAL UPLIFT, in order to BENEFIT THE VIEWER, THE READER, THE OBSERVER OR THE LISTENER.

**The world will become
peaceful, beautiful and abundant**

IF WE CONSTRUCT PLACES OF BEAUTY

We need to grow a new sensitivity to beauty on our planet. We are surrounded by eyesores which are reflections of our inner inability to heal - internal pain manifests externally. The landscape of our minds is reflected in the outer landscape.

Do we want to live in cramped, drab, concrete homes? Do we want our sight to be assaulted by a barrage of neon advertising signs? Do we want to tread on concrete all day long?

Do we want to be surrounded by dirt and decay? Do we want to live in places which are CARED FOR? If so, we must start to develop this care.

Aestheticism has been largely lost. Its decimation has been deliberate. We have attractive enclaves to which "tourists" flock, but such beauty spots should be commonplace - a universal phenomenon which occurs at every corner, instead of at the end of a long and expensive journey.

If we build a vision of a beautiful world in our hearts constantly, it will simultaneously be built in our physical surroundings.

**The world will become
peaceful, beautiful and abundant**

IF WE BUILD HOLY PLACES EVERYWHERE

This does not mean building more churches, mosques and temples which are visited once a week. There is no point in decorating our "holy places" in ornate gold, if others are starving. There is no point in voicing righteous rhetoric about the "brotherhood of man" if there are beggars lining the temple walls.

There is no point in praising Divinity if we fail to recognise the Divinity in ourselves and in all life.

It is not our mandate to labour in small, enclosed, suffocating spaces, creating limited harmony in locations to which one can temporarily "escape" if the "realities" of life prove too much to bear.

Holy places such as these are artificially built refuges to shelter the fearful and to feed the complacent.

It is time to shine our particular "light" OUTSIDE SUCH WALLS, and to recognise that

ALL PLACES ARE HOLY AND WORTHY OF OUR ATTENTION AND DEDICATION.

**The world will become
peaceful, beautiful and abundant**

IF WE COMBINE BEAUTY AND FUNCTIONALITY

If our hearts beat strongly at the sight of beauty, then may this inspire our creative actions. On the other hand, let us not "lose our heads" to beauty, but temper and regulate it with a view to functionality.

In a world where so many complex and antiquated structures DO NOT SERVE HUMANKIND, our future concepts MUST WORK.

Our beautiful visions must be tempered by practical considerations. Architects, engineers and artists will work hand in hand.

And to the same degree: if we are involved with "functional" projects, we should not forget to use our imagination and consider embellishment.

If we forgo the aesthetic aspect, we will produce a system or building which gives little joy. It may fulfil its purpose aptly, but it will not attract or uplift. This balance should be sought for mutual benefit.

CHAPTER 10

OUR RESPONSIBILITIES
TOWARDS RESOURCES AND
MATERIAL CREATIONS

**The world will become
peaceful, beautiful and abundant**

IF MATERIAL RESOURCES ARE WELL ORGANISED TO SERVE A COMMON GOAL

Great amounts of energy are wasted in personal vendettas or public competition against each other.

Fierce competition results in battles for resources, hoarding, corruption, manipulation and deception. While competition can be healthy, destruction is certainly not.

What are "material resources"?

Natural resources, scientific knowledge, material goods and human potential. All these can be optimally co-ordinated so that we work together towards a worthy common goal.

In addition, we can make it a habit to use less, and thus throw away less. Recycling – especially recycling our valuable material – has great merits, but AVOIDING HUGE PILE UPS OF RUBBISH IN THE FIRST PLACE is our primary concern.

**The world will become
peaceful, beautiful and abundant**

IF NOTHING IS COPYRIGHTED OR PATENTED

Although "individual rights" are rightly protected by copyright, copyright also makes it extremely difficult to SPREAD material, and this can have a very negative impact on humanity.

Similarly, patents for innovations will protect the interests of the original inventor, but will also prevent widespread implementation of new and beneficial technology. Instead of such technology being released for the general good, in-fighting occurs, and inventors are paid off or threatened by powerful agents who wish to retain dominance over their particular market.

Ideally, everything will be open source, with credit given to the inventor/composer/author. For this to work, the money system must fall. This means that everyone will give their services free of charge, and that everything will be free.

This would work (and does work on planets with a higher level of spirituality) if no one ever takes more than they need, and if everyone contributes daily to the functioning of society, using their own particular skill to help others.

**The world will become
peaceful, beautiful and abundant**

IF NOTHING EVER NEEDS TO BE REPAIRED

If things break, like an umbrella, do we throw it away and buy another? Does the idea of finding someone to repair it even enter our heads? Is it possible to develop a metal which never shows fatigue? Will the quality of housing improve so drastically that buildings never need renovation? Is quality the present yardstick in construction or production?

Are we destined to buy cheap clothing which quickly falls apart, so that we go out and buy more cheap clothing? Do we put up a wooden fence, because it is cheaper, instead of metal railing which never needs replacing? Or do we realise that we can grow our own fences by planting bushes and trees?

We have plundered the earth through our poor choices. We have lined the pockets of those who push quick, cheap, low quality products. We no longer value high quality products, or those which are handmade and unique. We have moved towards mass produced uniformity. We follow "fashion", which changes often to extract even more money. Planned obsolescence also ensures a rapid turnover of goods. All this is dishonest trade and a deplorable waste of resources. The answer is to ensure HIGH QUALITY AT EVERY TURN.

The world will become peaceful, beautiful and abundant

IF WE PRODUCE LASTING PRODUCTS BY BLENDING EXACTLY THE RIGHT MIX

Cement is a powder which flies, a liquid which flows, a paste which sticks and a solid which is incapable of change. It is used as a binding agent. But using it to cement objects together is not simply a matter of mixing it with water and applying it.

If we make a mistake, it is difficult to remove cement IF IT IS NOT DONE SO IMMEDIATELY, as it changes rapidly from powder, to porridge, to rock. We have to ACT VERY QUICKLY to put it in the appropriate places. So if we are distracted by something else, it sets solid. We must tidy up and wash up our tools IMMEDIATELY AND WITH DILIGENCE, otherwise our tools will quickly lose their SHARPNESS AND EFFECTIVENESS, which in its turn prevents us from doing QUALITY WORK.

Whatever the quality of our tool, a hesitant hand produces a hesitant uneven surface. Timing is important. If we use too much water at a late stage, the cement will shrink. If we do not clean our workplace properly, we will have to deal with it LATER.

We can compare the process of mixing and applying cement to the process of mixing and applying the TRUTH: we must apply exactly the right consistency, at exactly the right time, with exactly the right tools, to exactly the right surface, and we must be of exactly the right mind (and skill) set. Only then will corrections be permanent. Only then will "cement" take permanent hold. Only then will "truth" be understood.

**The world will become
peaceful, beautiful and abundant**

IF ACHIEVED PERFECTION IS MAINTAINED

Even if a building is constructed in accordance with a perfect "blueprint", it will fall into neglect if we do not look after it. Similarly, if the principle of maintenance is applied to ALL OUR COMPLETED IDEAS, PROJECTS AND PLANS, they will endure.

We all have a DIVINE BLUE-PRINT INHERENT IN OURSELVES. It is our task to fulfil it. We can ask ourselves "What dreams or measures have we set into motion but thereafter neglected?" or "How many unfinished projects are lying on our desks or are buried away in our cupboards?".

If these projects are worthy, and if they are in alignment with Divine law, they will be supported, yet we must initiate them, dedicate ourselves to them, and "maintain" them.

**The world will become
peaceful, beautiful and abundant**

IF WE PLAN PROJECTS WHICH LAST FOR A THOUSAND YEARS

Trying to unravel and understand the complex situation on earth, with a view to correcting it and providing positive future perspectives, is a mammoth task. How should we go about it? Firstly, it requires some very thorough and comprehensive investigation into WHAT HAS GONE WRONG. Only then can we understand how deep we have fallen. Then we can compare it to THE PERFECT SITUATION and determine what corrections are necessary. Possible solutions must be discussed with experts in diverse fields. Superficial changes will not be effective. Improvements must be permanent. Co-creative effort will strengthen all projects. Resources and high-quality materials must be used effectively, and never wasted.

While drawing up plans, we will continually assess whether they benefit everyone. IMMACULATE PLANNING is required, with emphasis on STRICT SAFETY PRECAUTIONS AND REGULATIONS. We will play it all through AS IF THE PROJECT IS GOING TO LAST A THOUSAND YEARS. This will highlight which elements are weak in the chain of command or in areas of production. We will proceed with absolute attention to detail, as well as keeping an overview. We will revise the situation continually during construction.

CHAPTER 11

OUR ENVIRONMENTAL
RESPONSIBILITIES

**The world will become
peaceful, beautiful and abundant**

IF WE NURTURE OUR EARTH
AS A LIVING BEING

For millennia, the earth has been viewed by the majority as a soulless machine. She has been overused, mistreated, disregarded, exploited and left to rust. Some parts have been removed, resulting in malfunction. How will we set about repairing this damage? Scattered and discarded parts of the "machine" need to be recovered, replaced or rebuilt. Rust must be pared away. Every cog must be lubricated to enable smooth movement. Every part must be cared for, and essential nuts and bolts must be tightened. Most important of all, programming must be reset in accordance with the highest benefit to earth and to humanity. Only thus can we repair our relationship with our benefactress.

All our relationships must be nurtured, especially our relationship with our MOTHER EARTH who is not actually a machine but a LIVING ORGANISM, and who has been left to suffer in extreme conditions without "food and water" for a very long time. Our earth is like a dried-out plant who will not recover immediately - she requires some time. She cannot process a huge bucket of water, thrown at her head immediately out of guilt, for most of this would sink immediately through her parched soil without being retained.

Instead, ensure that she is nourished continually in frequent small steps, like all relationships should be nourished. Encourage her to grow and to trust us once again. May we apologise for our atrocious behaviour which has caused her thirst and distress. May we live in gratitude that she has nurtured us for so long without complaint.

As we walk through our lives, may we be attentive to her. May we be as generous and forgiving as she has been. May we check regularly for pests which threaten her health. May we learn WHAT WENT WRONG so that we can correct our behaviour. May we show her love that she might heal.

**The world will become
peaceful, beautiful and abundant**

IF WE CHERISH BEAUTY

Do we cherish beauty 100% of the time? Or even 51% of the time? If we did, the scales would tip from chaos, torment, abuse and corruption into peace, abundance and harmony. But exactly what or who is beautiful? How often do we consider ourselves as important "pieces" in a beautiful global jigsaw? Are we aware that everyone has a starting point, and that everyone sets out on a journey, looking for similar pieces in order to "interlock" and form a composite and beautiful whole? It is time to conceive of OURSELVES as part of the BEAUTY.

**The world will become
peaceful, beautiful and abundant**

IF WE LEARN FROM NATURE

There are so many ways in which the natural world can help and inspire. Each tiny seed fulfils its own specific potential. This awe-inspiring process leads us to ask HOW CAN I ALSO REACH MY FULL POTENTIAL, ALIGNING WITH MY DIVINE PLAN?

Nature can inspire and strengthen our architecture – for example the stability of giant redwoods and bamboo, or the intricate hexagons in a bee's home. Nature gives us water which quenches our thirst, herbs which heal, fragrances which delight, fruits which nurture and a huge diversity of animal life to help us and provide companionship. Ants and bees who work together in communities are fascinating - a world far removed from life in a concrete jungle where one is unaware of the passing seasons.

When we see the OPPOSITE OF BEAUTY, it is easy to be depressed. How can we counteract this? In order to cherish beauty, we must CHERISH OURSELVES, and cherish the DIVINE PLAN. We must also cherish the POTENTIAL (however small) in everyone we meet, as well as in every flower and blade of grass. In addition, we should cherish all mistakes, for they are the fastest route to learning. We should also cherish everyone who has evoked our anger and awakened us to our real role, which is to be LOVE CRUSADERS.

**The world will become
peaceful, beautiful and abundant**

IF WE REVERSE OUR WASTE POLICIES

How often do we use wood, paper or water – and all other materials generously provided by our Earth – only to discard them immediately? There is very obvious widespread wastage, for example throwing away a paper cup after drinking ONE coffee. This could be considered a crime against our earth – our benefactress and a living organism. Imagine the energy, the construction, the transportation of the cup and then – following that ONE COFFEE-DRINKING MOMENT - the disposal, transport and (hopefully) "recycling" which follows. MILLIONS of cups are discarded in this fashion.

Millions of ironed shirts crumple the moment they are put on, and are discarded every day for a new one. Multiple rivers have been redirected or dammed, and now require RE-NATURALISATION. Forests have been decimated, and land has been polluted. These areas need RE-PLANTING and RE-HABILITATION. In addition, our poisoned bodies need COMPLETE DETOXIFICATION. All the self-created imbalances in our lives and in nature now require our UNDIVIDED ATTENTION. From a distance, one would consider this absolute MADNESS. This POLICY OF WASTE is a deliber-ate attempt to sabotage health and natural beauty, and it must be reversed by using less and giving up our squandering habits.

**The world will become
peaceful, beautiful and abundant**

IF WE TRANSFORM THE WORLD INTO A GARDEN

If our eyes are trained to recognise BEAUTY, and if they are also trained to recognise EYESORES, our awareness of both will increase. As a result, we will feel an intense urge to go out and BEAUTIFY OUR SURROUNDINGS as much as possible.

This extends from our personal space to the world outside, where human hand has played a large role in changing the landscape, whether this means building roads, buildings and factories, or whether this means altering topography and "natural areas" for agriculture or profit.

So far, manipulating our surroundings has often been the result of rational, functional or profit-making motivations. Our motivation has not been INCREASING BEAUTY.

This aspect should automatically be incorporated into every decision and project. Outdoors and indoors should merge and complement each other. Buildings will be put into nature, and nature will be put into buildings. This will be much more that putting a plant on the window-sill. Our mandate is to LIVE WITH NATURE AND TO CARE FOR IT.

**The world will become
peaceful, beautiful and abundant**

IF WE USE WHAT WE ALREADY HAVE

All over the world, we accumulate huge piles of trash. This can be due to lack of resources to deal with rubbish adequately, but often it results from a

LOW LEVEL OF CONSCIOUSNESSS.

Some people insist that everything has to be new, and thus they frequently replace things, with no thought whatsoever for the materials used, the effort required to make them, the energy involved in transport, or indeed the energy involved in their disposal.

The earth has been plundered for all sorts of materials which are deemed absolutely necessary for our well-being, but this can be reduced if we lower our "living standards". Where raw materials and water are scarce, and where there is a different mentality at play, such resources will be re-used again and again.

So, we are urged to open up our drawers, see what is in our cellars, and consider how all this can be USEFUL NOW, if not to us, then to others. In some cases, we will be astounded because we actually find things we just went out to buy. Thus will we make increasingly more use of what we have, and avoid unnecessary squandering.

**The world will become
peaceful, beautiful and abundant**

**IF EVERYONE TAKES ON
GUARDIANSHIP OF THE EARTH**

Who does the earth belong to? To HERSELF. Ideally, her inhabitants (temporary guests) will develop the awareness that they are not owners but GUARDIANS who are entrusted with looking after her resources and lands.

To partition land and put it under the guardianship of ALL individuals, with the possibility of passing it on to heirs as "inheritance", is positive in that it will encourage the younger generation, in their turn, to give their piece of land a higher level of care.

It will also encourage us to produce our own food, thus reducing the need to transport foodstuffs over long distances.

If everyone has a garden and produces a portion of their own food, there will be less need for huge monocultures, and no more need for an apple to travel a thousand miles before it is consumed. Local networks will be strengthened and joy will be gained from growing one's own food.

The world will become
peaceful, beautiful and abundant

IF WE INCREASE EMPATHY AND
UNDERSTANDING TOWARDS ALL THINGS

Can we understand a tree? Can we stand still and bear all weathers as trees do? Can we imagine hearing the approaching saws and not being able to run? Can we imagine dying as they do? Can we feel their sorrow and the pain of being wounded?

Can we feel the despair of those who lose children or families?

Can we understand the earth? Can we feel the pain we have inflicted and continue to inflict upon her body? Can we understand a star or another planet?

Can we imagine the waves emanating from our weapons of destruction reaching and deforming the atmospheres of other planets?

UNDERSTANDING does not happen in a casual encounter or split second. It is a long process involving unfailing concentration, patience, and a willingness to transfer attention away from oneself TOWARDS THE OTHER.

CHAPTER 12

OUR NATIONAL
AND GLOBAL
RESPONSIBILITIES

**The world will become
peaceful, beautiful and abundant**

IF EVERYONE IS CONSCIOUS OF THE WAVES THEY EMIT

Like a stone thrown into a pond, our soul lands in a body and immediately starts to cause ripples. We start to make decisions at a very early age. We learn that crying gets us some attention, even if, as a baby, we cannot explain what sort of attention we need. We also decide how long to scream, and when to stop, if no one comes. Whatever stage we are at - in babyhood or adulthood - we continue to "make waves", even if we are not conscious of doing so. When someone enters a room, or a life, the atmosphere changes. When they leave, it changes again.

We are the ones who determine the QUALITY of our actions. When we throw a stone into a pond, we decide the quality of those waves and WHERE THEY WILL SPREAD. If we do not act, the water will remain still, but "stillness" will also have an effect. Waves will continue ETERNALLY. Thought traverses the universe. Any "Waves" from nuclear detonations in our atmosphere also TRAVEL FAR, threatening other beings on other planets. To be always aware of the consequences of our actions, and to restrain from making wrong moves, is to ensure peace on our earth and good relations with our planetary neighbours.

**The world will become
peaceful, beautiful and abundant**

IF WE LOOK UPON OUR PETTY STRUGGLES FROM A POINT IN SPACE

Astronauts often return to earth with a feeling of wonder after seeing our beautiful spherical home from a distance. It is very obviously ONE WORLD, and from afar, it all seems in perfect order, although its atmosphere looks thin and fragile. At the same time, astronauts are aware of millions of people on the ground going about their daily lives, governed by the structures we have created for ourselves over millennia.

What will happen if we hold this view of our earth in our hearts on a daily basis? This is a perspective which rises above petty arguments and struggles, contemplations of what to wear, what menu to cook, what strategy to employ to impress, and what avenue to choose to succeed. Love for our earth - and concern for everyone on it - will prevail.

**The world will become
peaceful, beautiful and abundant**

IF WE EMBRACE UNITY

Perhaps the idea of OVERRIDING UNITY is very difficult to visualise on a planet where so many different (and fiercely defended) beliefs, customs and cultures reign.

HOW CAN WE PUT OUR DIFFERENCES ASIDE?

This requires active participation by every individual, and active release of all dogma, superstition and customs which do not serve humanity as a whole. When our faulty belief systems crumble, we will strive towards universal truths. We will be UNITED in our despair of having followed an erroneous path for so long: UNITED we shall also be in the tremendous new upsurge in our hearts and in our UNIVERSAL DEDICATION to improve, walking a new path towards UNIVERSAL HAPPINESS.

Corrective action must take place on all levels. As in all situations involving disaster, we will be drawn together and help one another. We will have so many questions that they will last a lifetime. We will rise out of stagnation and form real supportive communities. We will take on RESPONSIBILITY. We will UNITE, not only with each other but also with our animals and plants, knowing and treating them ALL as sentient and sensitive beings.

**The world will become
peaceful, beautiful and abundant**

IF PEOPLE RELEASE THEIR FEARS AND SHARE EVERYTHING

The desire to hoard things is an illness. It shows that we have lost faith that abundant opportunities will arise in the future. It assumes a "worst case scenario". It rejects the idea that life is divinely guided and that we will all be cared for like the "lilies growing in the field".

Hoarding money or material goods means that these assets remain in one place, when they could be doing good elsewhere.

This is STAGNANT ENERGY, which ideally should be FLOWING. Sometimes we want to "flow", for example we want to move to a new destination or house, but we are dragged down by the THINGS WE HAVE HOARDED, especially in the cellar and attic.

There was an investigation of some African villages some years ago. They all had the same problems, including locusts and unsafe water. But after a number of years, it was clear that one village was better off than all the rest. This was due to the fact that the villagers shared their produce instead of hoarding it for difficult times.

**The world will become
peaceful, beautiful and abundant**

IF WE FOCUS ON OUR SIMILARITIES

The fire of youth is highly commendable: it can move mountains, yet it can also usher us into high avenues of extremism, from which we may never be able to descend. In addition, there is a sense of pride at being different, as if this difference is what saves our sanity and which gives meaning to life.

But it is the differences which separate us, which make us look down upon another. All consciously aware humans strive in their relationships to be understood, and are deeply disappointed if they are not. Crises ensue from focussing on that which is different. This is riveted into our society on earth, and it has divided us into intense fighting factions: killing each other is on the agenda.

What degree of "difference" warrants attack? How did it come to this? If we harbour the feeling "I need to be understood", we are instantly on the lookout for those that do, and condemn those who don't, convinced that the latter will never be able to understand us. This is the fast track to war and self-annihilation. It is not our mandate to be understood but to seek to understand. This is a central pivot to catapult change. Individual families and the global family are split. The "generation gap" can be closed by seeking to understand rather than insisting on promoting supposed differences. This does not mean to say that we disrespect each person's unique qualities and character, it simply means that these unique qualities should be IMPLEMENTED to reach out to others, to inspire others, to make contact with all, rather than to make contact with only those who agree with our opinions.

The world will become peaceful, beautiful and abundant

IF WE FAVOUR ORGANISM OVER ORGANISATION

It is essential that we conceive of ourselves as one organism, with our earth being the torso, and us being the fingers or toes. In a body of perfect health, all cells and body parts will communicate incessantly and completely, without any blockages impeding the flow. Each cell knows its particular task and required contribution intuitively. It knows that solidarity is necessary for perfect functioning in times of peace and stillness, as well as for co-ordinating resistance against attack in times of "war" or illness.

Whatever the situation, the condition of every cell (and in our metaphor, this means the spiritual condition and mental health of every inhabitant of earth) affects the whole, and the combined effort of the whole will rise to the occasion without hesitation when necessary.

The world will become
peaceful, beautiful and abundant
IF WE INCREASE DEVOTION AND LOYALTY

Strong loyalty is generally restricted to family, or smaller social or religious groups. Marriage is a structure which requires loyalty and which - over the millennia - has contributed to increasing the stability of society. To extend this loyalty to a country or nation will prevent local or provincial "in-fighting". Some will call this patriotism, or even nationalism in a derogatory way, but irrespective of the labels we choose, this can be a positive phenomenon which consolidates self-confidence, and increases stability. Providing that mutual respect is maintained, A STABLE NATION IS CAPABLE OF STABLE RELATIONSHIPS WITH OTHER NATIONS.

The world will become
more peaceful, beautiful and abundant
IF ALL PEOPLE ARE STRENGTHENED BY
THEIR OWN CULTURE AND IDENTITY

This may sound like a sort of "segregation", but personal stability is necessary in order to have the poise, grace and confidence to encounter others in a calm and peaceful way. People like to know what their roots are and tend to feel "lost" when they are uprooted or forced to migrate. If we know without a doubt that our culture is valued and UNIQUE, we will be more capable of seeing other culture as valuable and UNIQUE.

**The world will become
peaceful, beautiful and abundant**

IF THERE IS A GENUINE COMMONWEALTH

If all countries have the feeling that they are associated under one umbrella or joint cause, this will bring about stability, not in the sense of one country dominating the others, as has been the case in the past, but in the sense that everyone is different but belongs to the same "family". This means that loosely associated states are allowed and encouraged to exercise internal autonomy, but that they are very aware of the fact that their neighbours have the right to do likewise.

The UNITED STATES OF AMERICA are an example of this, which could be expanded to

THE UNITED STATES OF AFRICA or

THE UNITED STATES OF ASIA, or indeed,

THE UNITED STATES OF THE WORLD.

**The world will become
peaceful, beautiful and abundant**

**IF ALL GLOBAL INHABITANTS
ACHIEVE A GLOBAL
OVERVIEW**

As we go about our duties every day, are we simultaneously aware of the old newspapers rotting away in our attic? The physical level is paralleled on the mental level. The things "at the back of our minds" require attention. On a global level, we are invited to be aware of deserts when we are in lush hills, to be aware of the massive power of the oceans when we are at the source of a river, to be aware of the huge differences in terrain, the huge differences of wealth and poverty, and the extreme differences between the advantaged and the disadvantaged.

Being aware of these differences continuously encourages feelings of gratitude in ourselves, and fuels the desire to instigate change. For those in dire circumstances, knowledge that there is so much more on this earth to experience will provide hope. Widening our perspectives is not always a pleasant process, but it is valuable gain a global overview will ultimately lead to abundance for all.

**The world will become
peaceful, beautiful and abundant**

IF WE REVERSE THE WASTEFUL AND EXPLOITATIVE ASPECTS OF GLOBALISATION

In poorer parts of the world, whole economies revolve around producing goods which are mainly for export - tee, coffee, bananas or flowers. As a result, areas of India or Africa are dependent on international demand and on "middle men" who make large profits by paying low wages.

This exploitation must stop. The land used to produce export goods will be used to grow food for the local populace. This means the end of indulging exotic tastes like importing flowers to Europe from Tanzania.

If we produce and buy products locally, we support and strengthen our own communities, avoid expensive transportation costs, learn to live in a simpler and more humble way, and improve communication and understanding on a local level.

**The world will become
peaceful, beautiful and abundant**

IF MIGRATING PEOPLE SHOW GENUINE INTEREST IN PEACEFUL INTEGRATION

Successful integration means getting used to another person, community or nation, so that everyone can co-exist and enrichen each other in a peaceful manner.

In a relationship, both partners must adjust. They cannot simply insist that their life as a "single" continues.

In a new community, a newcomer should first observe and learn how it functions. Only then can they assess whether it is a successful community or not, or what changes could be made for the benefit of the whole, or how they can personally best contribute.

In a new country, it is also necessary to observe, learn and seek common ground with a view to contributing to its stability.

**The world will become
peaceful, beautiful and abundant**

IF WE ALL SPEAK THE SAME LANGUAGE

The plethora of languages on this planet has hindered its evolution into a peaceful global community. We tend to feel closer to those who speak our own language.

A feeling of respect and kinship must be developed between all human beings, and language is a great unifying factor.

English is the obvious choice for this. Some people will immediately object to this suggestion because they love their "mother tongue" and value the culture of which it is part. They fear that this will be lost for ever.

But speaking a universal language does not necessarily mean "losing" great traditions or cultures; it means retaining the best of all traditions and cultures.

The world will become
peaceful, beautiful and abundant

IF REVOLUTION IS REPLACED BY EVOLUTION

The phrase "Where we go one, we go all" is relevant to this issue. With any group work (and this planet hosts a very large group of human beings), development can only take place at the pace of the slowest. This means that if there is someone who does not understand the topics or measures under discussion, then the forward movement of the whole is "hampered". On a larger scale, if those who understand (or think they understand) take action independently, without including the "slow learners", revolution will take place.

Including the "slow learners" is replacing revolution by evolution. If absolutely EVERYONE participates fully and is brought to grasp completely what is going on and why change is necessary, then the changes will be permanent, because they are firmly rooted in personal experience. This method is slower than revolution, but it is more effective in the long run.

How can this be achieved? Through continuous patient teaching and explanation by trusted "leaders". A "leader" or teacher only needs to be one step ahead to teach.

Flourishing trade, good relations and excellent mutual understanding between nations and peoples is possible if the most promising and enlightened leadership figures of each group are brought together for mutual learning. Later they can then return home with new knowledge which they can introduce to their own communities.

**The world will become
peaceful, beautiful and abundant**

**IF WE MAINTAIN PEACEFUL RELATIONS
WITH OUR GALACTIC NEIGHBOURS**

For thousands of years, earth has been a "prison planet" for souls which require rehabilitation. On earth, they have been given a chance – during a series of incarnations – to turn to the "light" and to develop altruistic tendencies. As such, earth has been closely observed by galactic administration to "contain" wayward behavior such as detonating nuclear bombs into the atmosphere. This has a negative effect on planetary neighbours. Once the extra-terrestrial presence and the true history of the "colonization" of earth has been revealed, it will be our task to improve our relations with our galactic neighbours after this long period of "quarantine". Although we are a very small, insignificant planet on the edge of our superuniverse, we have a significant role to play as an example of progress made, and in the development of future universes.

CHAPTER 13

OUR RESPONSIBILITY
TO THE FUTURE

**The world will become
peaceful, beautiful and abundant**

IF ITS INHABITANTS REALISE WE INCARNATE TO HAVE A SPIRITUAL EXPERIENCE

This is an evolutionary planet for the development of souls. Our bodies are merely the vehicle we use to have a spiritual experience, and it is this experience which we take with us on our eternal learning journey. Our concern for new and old souls reincarnating on earth, including ourselves, must be long-term, as opposed to the limited mind-set of thinking that this is the only life we have. We can have "eternal life" if we choose it (However, some souls are not capable of moral choice, which prevents them from going down this avenue) It is erroneous to believe that material things are our greatest concern. Our concern should ideally extend not only to the "fate" of children and grandchildren, but to all humanity eternally.

**The world will become
peaceful, beautiful and abundant**

IF WE KNOW WE ARE TAKING AN EXAMINATION IN AN ETERNAL CAREER

Periodically, cosmic energies of various sorts will bring present cycles to closure, and these points in time offer a "window" for enormous change. Earth wants to take advantage of this "window"; she no

172

longer wishes to be a carrier of violence, or a victim of abuse, and wants to move into a higher level of consciousness. We could also call this a "higher level of spirituality". Planetary inhabitants will be grouped according to whether they can move into this field of higher vibration, or whether they will have to leave and go to their next "school of learning" (in another life or on another planet). Some may also be at the end of their particular task on earth, and "drop" their bodies (known on earth as "death") to continue elsewhere. It is the quality of our behaviour which determines where we go - whether we pass the examination with flying colours, whether we barely scrape through it, or whether we fail dismally.

Some of us, unaware of universe administration and the eternal career, focus more on relaxing and enjoying ourselves. Because we think that this is our only life, we want to "make the most of it". However, it is not our life's purpose to languish and amuse ourselves with pointless or even harmful distractions. Nor is it our destiny to fall into lethargy, completing only those tasks which are absolutely necessary, responding only to outward pressures of force, doing the minimum instead of creating new exciting perspectives.

Our goal is not to play eternally, but to build and assist others on their journey, WHICH IS ALSO PART OF OUR JOURNEY, AS WE ARE ALL PART OF EACH OTHER.

**The world will become
peaceful, beautiful and abundant**

IF WE ARE ALWAYS AWARE OF DEATH

When we die, we take NOTHING with us, except that which we have LEARNT. We are on a

SPIRITUAL LEARNING JOURNEY

temporarily using a human body in order to have that experience.

In our material world today, so much focus is on wealth accumulation and material goods, as well as on outward appearances. WHATEVER WE DO, we will not be able to keep "good looks" or our youthful bodies.

To be in constant denial (and to be constantly taking measures to counteract something which is inevitable) is pointless and unauthentic. It is sending energy in a "selfish" direction, to no avail in the long run.

To be constantly aware of death - which is actually just going through another door to another room - is to live intensely and authentically.

**The world will become
peaceful, beautiful and abundant**

IF WE ARE AWARE OF ETERNITY

If we are aware of eternity, we will realise that collecting wisdom, skills and experiences is more important than anything else, and we will regard our body as a vehicle for the soul, rather than as a show-case to attract other show-cases.

To be aware of eternity means forging friendships, learning from encounters and incidents, and moving on without drama or regret to new friends and new encounters. There will always be another horizon, a new chance, a new offer of fulfilment, a new challenge, and a new joy. We never "lose" anyone, because they are on their eternal journey too, and our paths will cross again.

Knowledge of eternity shows us the futility of wars, for battles can never be "won". Death is not necessarily the end. We all survive "death", if we choose to continue to learn. After "death" we remember, and from this new perspective, we understand our learning experiences. These will determine our next learning steps. To be aware of eternity means having an unshakeable belief in one's own potential to develop, to increasingly show unconditional love and to excel in creative acts. To do all this, and to learn to live in continuous joy, we have all the time in the world, and in the next.

LIST OF STATEMENTS

CHAPTER 1:
OUR RESPONSIBILITY TO
REGULATE OUR BEHAVIOUR

**The world will become
peaceful, beautiful and abundant**

IF WE LOOK INTO EACH OTHER'S EYES
IF EVERYONE PAUSES TO THINK BEFORE
THEY SPEAK
IF WE THROW AWAY THE PROPS AND SMILE
IF WE TREAT EVERYONE WE ENCOUNTER
WITH CONSIDERATION
IF WE SHOW COURTESY, GRATITUDE AND
COMPASSIONATE HONESTY
IF WE DEVELOP PATIENCE WHERE IT IS DUE
IF WE DO NOT IMMEDIATELY JUDGE
IF EVERYONE RECOGNISES THAT WHAT
THEY SEE IS A MIRROR OF THEMSELVES
IF WE INCREASE THE QUALITY WE PERCEIVE
IS LACKING IN OTHERS
IF EVERYTHING IS PROCESSED
IMMEDIATELY
IF WE TRANSCEND THE PAST
IF WE INCREASE DEVOTION AND LOYALTY
IF WE ARE COURAGEOUS TO THE CORE
IF WE LEARN TRUE TRUST
IF WE PRACTICE TRUE HUMILITY
IF WE RETAIN ETERNAL, CENTRAL REPOSE

CHAPTER 2:
OUR RESPONSIBILITY TO KEEP LEARNING

**The world will become
peaceful, beautiful and abundant**

IF WE REGARD OBSTACLES AS CHANCES TO
MOVE FORWARD
IF WE TAKE ENOUGH TIME TO THINK DEEPLY
IF WE DO NOT RUN ON AUTOMATIC
IF WE DEPROGRAMME OURSELVES
IF WE JOURNEY IN EVER-WIDENING CIRCLES
IF WE GO INTO ACTION INSTEAD OF HIDING
BEHIND WORDS
IF WE KEEP ON TRACK DESPITE ATTEMPTS
TO DISRUPT US
IF WE CONTINUALLY CHECK GROWTH AND
KEEP EVERYTHING IN VIEW
IF WE STOP IGNORING VIOLENCE, UGLINESS
AND DESECRATION
IF WE REMEMBER TO KEEP EVERYTHING IN
OUR VISION
IF EVERYONE RESEMBLES A DIAMOND
IF WE LEARN TO FALL, AND FALL TO LEARN
IF EVERYONE KNOWS THAT THEY DO NOT
KNOW
IF WE REMEMBER THERE IS SO MUCH MORE
WE DON'T KNOW
IF WE RECOGNISE THE END
IF WE TRACK OUR ACTIVITIES
IF WE RECOGNISE THE GREAT TEACHERS
AMONG US

CHAPTER 3:

OUR RESPONSIBILITY TO MANIFEST OUR VISIONS

The world will become peaceful, beautiful and abundant

IF BEAUTIFUL THOUGHTS ARE ACTED UPON
IF WE TRY TO TURN OUR VISIONS INTO
REALITY
IF HUMANS RISE ABOVE THEIR PRESENT
CONCEPT OF THEMSELVES
IF WE GO BEYOND THE BOUNDARIES OF THE
FAMILIAR
IF WE CAN IMAGINE THE IMPOSSIBLE
IF WE KNOW WHAT TO KEEP AND WHAT TO
DESTROY WHILE CREATING OUR DREAM
IF WE KEEP OUR EYES ON OUR GOAL
IF WE STOP KNOCKING OUR HEADS AGAINST
A BRICK WALL
IF WE PRODUCE OUR OWN ECSTATIC
EXPERIENCES WITHOUT DRUGS
IF WE LIVE THE GREATEST VERSION OF
OURSELVES

CHAPTER 4:

**OUR RESPONSIBILITY
TO ACHIEVE TRUE TRANSPARENCY**

**The world will become
peaceful, beautiful and abundant**

IF WE KEEP THINGS SIMPLE
IF WE UNDERSTAND THAT EVERY MOMENT
IS UNIQUE
IF WE REALISE THAT SOME THINGS ARE THE
SAME
IF WE EMBRACE TRANSPARENCY AND
OPENNESS
IF WE CONTINUALLY CLEAR THE SPACE
WITHIN US
IF WE RELEASE OUR FEARS AND SHARE
EVERYTHING
IF WE CLEAR THE JUNGLE IN OUR MINDS
AND IN OUR WORLD
IF EVERYONE IS AWARE OF THE DECISION-
MAKING PROCESS IN EVERY SECOND
IF WE REALISE THAT OUTER VIRUSES ARE A
MIRROR OF INNER VIRUSES
IF WE RELEASE NEW TECHNOLOGY FOR THE
BENEFIT OF ALL

CHAPTER 5:

OUR RESPONSIBILITY TO INCREASE PERSONAL SOVEREIGNTY AND INDEPENDENCE

The world will become peaceful, beautiful and abundant

IF WE CONQUER SELF-SABOTAGE
IF WE DECLINE THE SPECIAL OFFERS
IF WE DO NOT SUFFOCATE OURSELVES
IF WE CUT OUT THE MIDDLEMEN
IF WE STOP FOLLOWING BLINDLY
IF WE STOP TAKING PART IN THE THEATRE OF THE ABSURD
IF STAR SEEDS COME OUT OF HIDING
IF EVERYONE IS CONTINUALLY AWARE OF THEIR DECISION-MAKING
IF WE REALISE THAT THE INSIDE DETERMINES THE OUTSIDE
IF WE DO NOT WAIT FOR COLLAPSE
IF WE REALISE OUR GODLY POWER

CHAPTER 6:

OUR DIVINE RESPONSIBILTIES

The world will become peaceful, beautiful and abundant

IF WE REALISE THAT WE CANNOT GET AWAY
WITH ANYTHING
IF WE KNOW WHO WE ARE
IF WE LIVE THE GREATEST POSSIBLE
VERSION OF OURSELVES
IF PEOPLE DO NOT COMPARE, AND IF THEY
TRUST IN THE DIVINE
IF WE SPREAD THE DIVINE PART OF
OURSELVES
IF WE CONSTANTLY REMEMBER THE
GOLDEN RULE: WE REAP WHAT WE SOW
IF WE REALISE THAT WE ARE ONE,
AND ONE IS ALL
IF WE REALISE THAT WE ARE EVERYTHING
IF THE WHOLE LANDSCAPE IS SURVEYED
IF WE HOLD THE WHOLE SPECTRUM IN OUR
MINDS DURING SIMPLE PROCESSES
IF WE ARE ALWAYS IN THE FLOW
IF WE CAN STOP FOCUSSING ON TIME
IF WE LOOK INSIDE FOR THE ANSWERS
IF WE CHOOSE LIGHT OVER DARK
IF WE CHOOSE TO LOSE IN ORDER TO WIN
IF WE EXPAND OUR IDEA OF GOD
IF WE EMBRACE THE ABSOLUTE

CHAPTER 7:

OUR RESPONSIBLITIES IN RELATIONSHIPS

**The world will become
peaceful, beautiful and abundant**

IF MAN AND WOMAN TRULY COMPLEMENT
AND RESPECT EACH OTHER

IF THE RIFT BETWEEN MAN AND WOMAN IS
HEALED

IF WE TRANSITION FROM I MATTER TO WE
MATTER

IF WE LOVE OUR CHILDREN
UNCONDITIONALLY FROM THE VERY
MOMENT OF CONCEPTION

IF WE PAY ATTENTION TO THE REQUESTS OF
OTHERS

IF WE ARE PREPARED TO TAKE TIME TO
REPAIR OUR RELATIONSHIPS

IF WE PEER INTO EACH OTHER'S SOULS

CHAPTER 8: OUR SOCIAL RESPONSIBILITIES

The world will become peaceful, beautiful and abundant

IF EVERYONE WORKS

IF WE OVERCOME COMPLACENCY

IF WE ARE UNDIVIDED IN OUR LOYALTIES

IF WE GIVE PRAISE WHERE PRAISE IS DUE

IF EDUCATION IS REPLACED BY EDUCATING

IF THE NEXT GENERATION IS EDUCATED BY A REVISED CURICULUM

IF WE SHOW TOTAL COMMITMENT TO THE WELFARE OF OTHERS

IF PEOPLE REALISE THAT CURING THEM-SELVES IS SIMULTANEOUSLY CURING OTHERS

IF EVERYONE BECOMES A PILLAR OF SOCIETY

IF WE ALL COMMIT TO A FORM OF PUBLIC SERVICE

IF RISKS ARE ELIMINATED AND COSTS AVOIDED

IF WE DEVELOP PERFECT SYNCHRONICITY

IF WE EMULATE BEES

IF WE TREAT ANIMALS AS WE TREAT OURSELVES

IF EVERYONE JOINS A CHOIR

IF WE REWRITE EARTH'S GENETIC MIND

IF WE CONTROL AND IMPROVE OUR GENETICS

CHAPTER 9:
OUR CULTURAL RESPONSIBILITIES

The world will become
peaceful, beautiful and abundant

IF MUSIC IS CONTINUALLY USED TO UPLIFT,
NURTURE AND COMFORT
IF MORE FORMS ARE ROUND
IF WE BECOME AWARE OF THE POWER OF
COLOUR
IF SPORT REGAINS ITS TRUE SIGNIFICANCE
IF WE CULTIVATE AND CELEBRATE BEAUTY
IN THE ARTS
IF WE CONSTRUCT PLACES OF BEAUTY
IF WE BUILD HOLY PLACES EVERYWHERE
IF WE COMBINE BEAUTY AND
FUNCTIONALITY

CHAPTER 10: OUR RESPONSIBILITIES
TOWARDS RESOURCES AND MATERIAL
CREATIONS

The world will become
peaceful, beautiful and abundant

IF MATERIAL RESOURCES ARE WELL
ORGANISED TO SERVE A COMMON GOAL
IF WE LIVE WITHOUT COPYRIGHTS, PATENTS
AND MONEY
IF NOTHING EVER NEEDS TO BE REPAIRED
IF WE PRODUCE LASTING PRODUCTS BY

BLENDING EXACTLY THE RIGHT MIX
IF ACHIEVED PERFECTION IS MAINTAINED
IF WE PLAN PROJECTS WHICH LAST FOR A
THOUSAND YEARS

CHAPTER 11:
OUR ENVIRONMENTAL RESPONSIBILITIES

**The world will become
peaceful, beautiful and abundant**

IF WE NURTURE OUR EARTH AS A LIVING
BEING
IF WE CHERISH BEAUTY
IF WE LEARN FROM NATURE
IF WE REVERSE OUR WASTE POLICIES
IF WE TRANSFORM THE WORLD INTO A
GARDEN
IF WE USE WHAT WE ALREADY HAVE
IF EVERYONE TAKES ON GUARDIANSHIP OF
THE EARTH
IF WE INCREASE EMPATHY AND
UNDERSTANDING TOWARDS ALL THINGS

CHAPTER 12: OUR NATIONAL AND GLOBAL RESPONSIBILITIES

The world will become peaceful, beautiful and abundant

IF EVERYONE IS CONSCIOUS OF THE WAVES
THEY EMIT
IF WE LOOK UPON OUR PETTY STRUGGLES
FROM A POINT IN SPACE
IF WE EMBRACE UNITY
IF PEOPLE RELEASE THEIR FEARS AND
SHARE EVERYTHING
IF WE FOCUS ON OUR SIMILARITIES
IF WE FAVOUR ORGANISM OVER
ORGANISATION
IF WE INCREASE DEVOTION AND LOYALTY
IF ALL PEOPLE ARE STRENGTHENED BY
THEIR OWN CULTURE AND IDENTITY
IF THERE IS A GENUINE COMMONWEALTH
IF ALL GLOBAL INHABITANTS ACHIEVE A
GLOBAL OVERVIEW
IF WE REVERSE THE WASTEFUL AND
EXPLOITATIVE ASPECTS OF GLOBALISATION
IF MIGRATING PEOPLE SHOW GENUINE
INTEREST IN PEACFUL INTEGRATION
IF WE ALL SPEAK THE SAME LANGUAGE
IF REVOLUTION IS REPLACED BY EVOLUTION
IF WE MAINTAIN PEACEFUL RELATIONS WITH
OUR GALACTIC NEIGHBOURS

CHAPTER 13:
OUR RESPONSIBILITY TO THE FUTURE

The world will become
peaceful, beautiful and abundant

IF ITS INHABITANTS REALISE THAT THIS IS
AN EVOLUTIONARY PLANET WHERE SOULS
INCARNATE IN THE PHYSICAL FOR A
SPIRITUAL EXPERIENCE

IF WE KNOW WE ARE TAKING AN
EXAMINATION IN AN ETERNAL CAREER

IF WE ARE THOROUGH

IF WE ARE ALWAYS AWARE OF DEATH

IF WE ARE AWARE OF ETERNITY

ART - MUSIC - SERAPHIN MESSAGES - SEMINARS

Rosie Jackson is author, artist, composer and founder of *The Spiritual Revolution Project*. This encompasses paintings, music, videos, books and seminars to develop self-awareness. Teaching spiritual principles to promote consciousness, her music and art are powerful catalysts of spiritual uplift. Her *Unity Tarot* illustrates the transformation of 100 global villagers in 2 large paintings and 100 written biographies.

Since 2010, Rosie Jackson has been receiving telepathic messages and visions from the angel, Seraphin. These various communications urge us to protect our earth and show us how paradise on earth can be achieved. The messages are presently available in English, German, Italian, Spanish, Dutch and Korean.

Born in England, Rosie Jackson studied German and French and qualified as a teacher. She has worked as an instructor in China, and as translator, designer and editor for publishing houses and companies in Europe. She now works freelance in Germany and Italy. rosie@rosiejackson.de.

WORKS BY ROSIE JACKSON

Compilations of Seraphin Messages in English,
German, Italian, Dutch and Spanish, from 2010 to 2019
The Unity Tarot in English and German, Parts 1 and 2
The Seraphin Prophecies and *Mediation Visions*
These can be downloaded at
http://www.rosie-jackson.de/pages/e_links.html

PUBLICATIONS BY ROSIE JACKSON

Seraphin's Spirituality School
ISBN 978-3-749485-84-0
The Peace Parables
ISBN 9783750441514
**The Absolutely Amazing Activity Book
of Snakes, Stars and Snowballs**
ISBN 978-3-8370-0238-6
**Wie das Schweinchen Prinzessin Prunella
das Lachen lernte**
ISBN 978-3-749428-85-4
**Ich bin Lebendigkeit:
Eine Reise zu mehr Authentizität, Kraft und Freude**
ISBN 978-3937883-32-8. EchnAton Publishers

ROSIE JACKSON: WEBSITES

ART: www.rosiejackson.de
SEMINARS: http://www.rosie-
jackson.de/revolution/Seminar_Termine.html
SERAPHIN MESSAGES:
www.rosiejackson.de/Seraphin
THE SPIRITUAL REVOLUTION PROJECT:
http://www.rosie-jackson.de/revolution/Projekt_und_Vision.html
YOUTUBE MUSIC/ARTVIDEOS
https://www.youtube.com/chanel/UCMCeJnqJ9Y7hqAExYmm9iKA

Rosie Jackson

AN ANGEL SPEAKS
SERAPHIN'S SPIRITUALITY SCHOOL
YOUR DIVINE ROLE:
CREATING AN ERA OF PEACE

ISBN 978-3-749485-84-0. 2019. 292 pages

Seraphin is an angel who send us messages of hope and inspiration, as well as practical advice. Our world requires a drastic makeover, and this will be fueled by a universal change of heart, by widening our perspectives, and by reconnecting to the divine core within us, which impels us to develop our skills in service to humanity. Seraphin's statements provide remarkable insights, provoke intense reflection, and challenge our limited viewpoint. With great clarity, he points out the necessity for radical change, while knowing that we have the power to implement it. The messages in this book were received telepathically by Rosie Jackson.

SERAPHIN'S SPIRITUALITY SCHOOL

This collection of 111 Seraphin Messages has 5 purposes. The first chapter, "Messages from the other side" encourage readers to start a writing journey, contacting their unseen guides and "downloading" information relevant to your particular task on earth.

As your spiritual abilities progress, you will increase in confidence, and you will become a source of inspiration for others.

Secondly, the chapters entitled "Your divine purpose", "Transcending your past", "Creating your future", and "Your relationships", intend to help readers along the spiritual path, assisting them to develop potential, achieve excellency, and use these skills and knowledge for the benefit of all.

Chapter 3, "Preparing for transition", provides advice on how to deal with the intense times ahead. Due to our present position in the photon belt, our planet is showered with highly powered cosmic energies. These create enormous change, supporting everything of divine nature, and exposing that which is not.

Fourthly, the chapters on rebuilding our world offer instructions on how to address practical problems. They also highlight which qualities we should manifest in order to maintain peace, beauty and abundance on our world.

Fifthly, the goal of the very last chapter, "Reconnecting to the universe", aims to increase our awareness of our galactic neighbours who lovingly observe us. After millennia of "disconnection", we will finally resume our membership of the cosmic family.

YOU ARE IN SPIRITUALITY SCHOOL

Seraphin Message 253: Through Rosie, 29th Jan. 2016

Despite the glory or the depravity of the physical surroundings in which you live, despite the physicality of your body and the need to attend to cleanliness and bodily functions, despite the physical motions you go through on a daily basis – all this is a

MEANS TO EXPERIENCE

rather than

THE AIM OF EXPERIENCE.

If you are fixated on these, you will always be mentally leaning towards your next physical "fix", whether it be the next meal or the next massage or the next sporting event or the next piece of advice or the next sexual encounter. On the physical level, this is an endless series of events, progressing in a linear fashion.

We ask you to consider that there is more to life than this, and in fact there is MORE LIFE in the sense that it does not simply stop after this incarnation.

If your mind is enslaved (and there are powers who would like to keep you in this position and who are very successful in their efforts to dupe you), if your mind is continually focusing on the next coffee, the next drug or entertainment slot, as in addiction, then there is

NO ROOM FOR GROWTH.

We do not mean growth in the physical sense but in the spiritual sense. Once deprived of your normal routine of "back to back" pleasures, as will surely come to pass in the next inevitable period of chaos on your world, you will be left with a VOID which you may be desperate to fill, or desperate to ignore.

To do so would be to deny your own growth as a divine being. To do so would be to reject the glory of choosing the much referenced and renowned "ETERNAL LIFE" (quoted in your holy books), offered to all who wish to climb the spiritual ladder.

This is an offer to take part in the truly huge and organised undertaking which is the administration and development and improvement and growth and prosperity of the entire universe – a scenario still hidden from your physical eyes, and yet you are part of it.

To repeat; you are not at a party, or on a battlefield, or in a playground, or in a one-time career; you are in a CLASSROOM. This life represents one class in an endless succession of educational institutions, whether on an evolutionary planet such as earth, whether on larger and more significant spheres, or beyond.

Yet all experiences are significant and contribute to the WHOLE, including your experience HERE ON EARTH where so many detours and deviations from the DIVINE TEMPLATE have taken place.

Your physical experience is a challenge of how to find the divine in a quagmire of corruption and deception; and when you have discovered that uplifting factor which benefits ALL, it is your specific task to

DEMONSTRATE THAT QUALITY, to

RISE ABOVE THE PHYSICAL PLANE

and to realise that you are both teacher and student in the UNIVERSAL SCHOOL OF SPIRITUALITY.

Rosie Jackson

THE PEACE PARABLES:
HOW THE FOOL BECAME GOD
AND OTHER STORIES

ISBN 9783750441514
140 pages. 2020

What do the stories with the titles INSIDE THE MARBLE and THE ROOF and THE EMERGENCY BRAKE have in common? Like the other 53 stories in this volume, they are "peace parables" because they urge us to improve our behaviour, not only for our own benefit, but for the common good, enabling us to co-create a peaceful world. Most of these parables are descriptions of visions received during meditation by the author, Rosie Jackson. Some are adaptations of messages received telepathically from the angel, Seraphin.

One of the most famous storytellers is the soul we call Jesus. Parables are an excellent way of teaching, as they entertain and educate people of various paths simultaneously, without raising an accusing finger. No one is addressed personally. It is up to readers to draw their own conclusions.

All these parables are designed to assist readers on their spiritual journey, opening up new vistas, opportunities and directions. The stories provide insights, shake up superstitions, encourage heroic acts, expose corruption, pinpoint our enslaved mentalities, reveal our debilitating dependence, revive our dormant creative powers, invite reassessment of the "status quo", reveal downward spirals, discourage materialism, inspire love of nature and foster true values.

The stories entertain and educate, urging us to search for better solutions, to clarify our choices, to increase our compassion and recognise our interconnection. They illuminate dangerous domino effects in our society today. They expose our narrowmindedness and blind allegiance. Most importantly, the stories are able to show us "another way", preparing us to be flexible in the face of great change, and forcing us to reflect upon that which is of supreme importance: OUR LIFE'S PURPOSE.

Rosie Jackson

THE ABSOLUTELY AMAZING ACTIVITY BOOK OF SNAKES, STARS AND SNOWBALLS

FURTHERING CREATIVE EXPRESSION IN CHILDREN FROM THE AGE OF 7 UP

ISBN: 978-3-8370-0238-6

Each of these 80 pages presents a story, idea, or situation which stimulates children's imagination through questions, suggestions or invitations to wonder what happens next.

The pictures they then draw are subconscious images of their inner world, feelings and desires, thus providing their carers with a valuable window to their soul.

Once children are accustomed to expressing their own emotions and needs, they are better able to assess themselves and others on the path towards mutual understanding and peace.

Like SNAKES they can shed their old skins, like SNOWBALLS they can move on and grow, reaching more and more towards the stars.